FEARS & PHOBIAS

FIGHTING BACK

by Neal Olshan and Julie Dreyer Wang

Franklin Watts/New York/London/
Toronto/Sydney/1980

*This book is dedicated to our
children: Sandy Olshan,
Timmy Wang, Bobby Olshan,
Kate Wang, and
Maureen Olshan*

Library of Congress Cataloging in Publication Data

Olshan, Neal.
　　Fears and phobias.

　　Bibliography: p.
　　Includes index.
　　SUMMARY: Distinguishes between normal and unreasonable fears and presents suggestions for overcoming phobias.
　　1. Fear—Juvenile literature. 2. Phobias—Juvenile literature. [1. Fear. 2. Phobias] I. Wang, Julie Dreyer, joint author. II. Title.
BF575.F2045　　　　　　152.4　　　　　　79–24044
ISBN 0–531–02865–8

"Sick" from *Where the Sidewalk Ends: The Poems and Drawings of Shel Silverstein.* Copyright © 1974 by Shel Silverstein. By permission of Harper & Row, Publishers, Inc.

Contents

Introduction 1

1. What Am I Afraid Of? 7

2. Will I Be Sick for School Today? 18

3. Fear of Not Making Friends 31

4. Fear of Doctors, Dentists, and Hospitals 43

5. Animal Fears and Phobias 56

6. Fear of Travel 66

7. Nightmares and Things That Go
   Bump in the Night 72

8. The Two-Sided Fear: Failure and Winning 80

9. Fear of Death, Divorce, and Separation 86

10. Now It's Up to You 92

    Appendix 103

    Selected Readings 118

    Index 119

Introduction

No matter how brave you are, there are times when you are going to be afraid. This book will help you understand which of your fears are normal and natural. It will also help you realize when your fears are getting the best of you. When this happens—when fears become exaggerated and unreasonable—they are called "phobias." Reading this book will teach you to overcome any phobias you may have and will make it easier for you to live a happier, more relaxed life.

How can you tell which fears you need help with? Well, you'd be crazy *not* to be afraid of sharks or lions, of crossing a busy street, or climbing a steep mountain. These fears help keep you alive. You also have some fears that are a natural part of growing up. As a baby you probably cried when mother left the room. You were afraid she had left you forever. But gradually you learned to master this fear by keeping an eye on her, crawling around after her, and then finally crawling away from her by yourself.

As children get older they learn to be separated

from their mothers for longer and longer periods of time. They do this by keeping a sense of mother with them, even though she is physically absent. They learn from experience to trust that mother will come back.

But let's say your mother were to leave you for an unusually long period of time, such as a vacation. Again, you might be afraid that mother will never come back and that you will be alone and hungry forever. This fear, which you first experienced at a very young age, will tend to return anytime your mother is away for a long period of time, or whenever you are tense or under stress. Even though you no longer need your mother as much as you did when she first went away, you still might feel sick to your stomach and afraid of being abandoned. In this way, a normal childhood fear, which you should have outgrown, can be turned into an exaggerated fear, or phobia.

Another natural fear during early childhood is a fear of strangers. By about eight months of age, an infant has learned to recognize mother and father. At first a baby may be happy to see a strange man, expecting him to be father. Suddenly the infant realizes that this is not father and cries, from fear or disappointment. Parents can and usually do comfort a child to help overcome this fear. However, if you had an unusually frightening experience with a stranger at a young age, you may still become excessively frightened by similar events, such as separations or meetings with strangers. This is another normal fear which can become an abnormal one.

During the years from four to six, you may develop fears arising from your love of mother, if you are a boy, or of father, if you are a girl. It is part of what is called the "oedipal" stage of development. During this time, a boy often experiences romantic feelings towards his mother and thinks he wants to marry her when he grows up. But he is also afraid that his father will be angry with him for loving his mother. Since a boy needs his father's approval and his example of how to grow into a man, he is torn between love and fear of his father. This conflict can give rise to anxieties and phobias, especially a fear of being hurt physically.

The problem is similar for a girl. For her, mother is a competitor for father's love and also a necessary model for growing up to be a woman. The conflict of not knowing whether she loves or hates her mother can lead to fear of being in an accident, or of something happening to her mother. If the conflict is strong enough, this fear will become an obsession. Fears such as these become much harder to get rid of as you get older and can stay with you long after you have grown out of this stage of your development.

Fears also may be displaced from one event or object to another. This means that although you are actually afraid of father, for example, you may transfer this fear to other powerful people, such as teachers or policemen. Fears can also be generalized. A child who is afraid of heights may develop fears of elevators, escalators, even tall buildings, or trees. Fears can have other symbolic meanings. Fear of heights may reflect fear of loss of control, loss of power, or even anger. It is often useful to think about the meaning and origins of a fear in order to overcome it.

Not all fear is bad, of course. A little fear adds spice to life. Skiing down a steep and difficult mountain is exhilarating and exciting precisely because it is dangerous and difficult. Our feeling of joy when we succeed comes, in part, from the realization that we have overcome our fear and reached the bottom safely.

Fear can also sharpen our minds and make our bodies function more efficiently. It triggers the release of adrenaline from our kidneys. Adrenaline is the most powerful stimulant in the body. It speeds up the heartbeat, constricts external blood vessels so that more blood is available for the brain, relaxes the lungs so that we can get more oxygen into our blood, and stops digestion, so that all our energies can be concentrated into "fight or flight."

Fight or flight is the term psychologists use to describe the survival instinct. When facing fierce animals, cavemen didn't have guns or nets or poison darts. They had to rely on one of two things—their ability to stay and fight it out with the animal, or the speed with which they could escape from danger. In either case, the release of adrenaline caused by their fear enabled them to fight more fiercely or run faster.

In the twentieth century, we no longer face wild animals. Most of our immediate needs, such as food, clothing, and shelter, are readily available, and we can't solve our problems by fighting or running away. Yet our fight-or-flight response remains, and it causes us to feel fear about things that are really emotional problems—such concerns as not having enough parental love, of being abandoned, or of failing in school. The fight-or-flight response is not very useful anymore, and it can be harmful. If it is triggered too often, it can cause ulcers and high blood pressure and also make us feel very uncomfortable. So it's important for good health to learn to control fear as much as possible.

Of course, you are not alone with your fears. Just about all of us grow up feeling sick to our stomachs, tense and panicky when faced with certain situations. In fact, fear is so common that we all have occasional fears of the dark or of thunder, for example. But one should outgrow such childhood fears as one grows older. The fears you have to work at getting rid of are the ones that keep cropping up over and over again— the ones you can't seem to outgrow, no matter how much you tell yourself not to be afraid.

The first step in getting over such fears and phobias is to admit to yourself that you have them. Pushing them to the back of your mind and pretending that nothing is bothering you isn't going to work for long. If your fears are getting in the way of a normal life, if you find yourself thinking and worrying about your fears a great deal, if you avoid certain situations to avoid facing your fears, then it's time to do something about them.

In this book, we will explain how to cope with your fears, and you will be amazed at how much smaller they seem. This book will also teach you how to relax, which helps a lot, because most fears are the results of unpleasant experiences, combined with a vivid imagination that allows you to anticipate the worst. By training your mind and body to relax and anticipate the best, instead of the worst, you can learn to overcome fear.

Getting rid of fears and phobias through relaxation and mind-training is the first step toward living a happier, more enjoyable life. Beyond that, you will need to discuss your fears with your parents, or with some other understanding adult who will be able to reassure you.

If fears persist in spite of your efforts to overcome them by relaxation and asking for friendly help, you might seek professional help. Therapists and psychiatrists help people understand and conquer fears in many ways. Sometimes dreams show us the origins of our fears, making them more manageable. Storytelling or acting out a fear also can make it understandable and easier to manage. Even fairytales, which are filled with frightening events, can help us find ways of overcoming our fears. In therapy, a child may find ways to communicate and master fears and get rid of many anxieties and feelings of discomfort.

Whatever your fears are, don't ignore them. There are many people willing and able to help you, but you must be the one to reach out and ask for help. No one can help you unless you want to be helped. Picking out this book has been the first, important step on your part that shows you really do want to work on your fears. So read on, and find out what you are afraid of, what you can do about it, and how you can stop fears and phobias from ruining your life.

1
What Am I Afraid Of?

Everyone is afraid sometimes. It's the most natural thing in the world to be afraid of fierce animals, deep water, high places, or dangerous criminals. These fears help you survive dangerous situations. Fear is like an "on" switch in your body. It triggers a series of reactions to make your heart beat faster, your muscles move more rapidly, your brain react quicker—to get you out of frightening situations.

But some children and adolescents become abnormally afraid of things they shouldn't be frightened of, such as dogs, cats, elevators, or the dark. Some exaggerate the normal apprehension that everyone feels before taking a test. So they may get sick or dizzy at the thought of going to school. They beg their mothers to let them stay at home before a test. Some adolescents stutter and feel embarrassed if they have to talk in front of the class. But gradually, with reassurance from your parents, you outgrow these fears—unless they get out of control.

Let's say you are afraid of cats. You were badly

scratched when you were very young, and you fear the same thing will happen again. So you spend a lot of time worrying about meeting cats on the way to school. You find yourself avoiding friends who have cats in their houses. Or you make excuses to cover up your real fear, because you are afraid people will laugh at you.

Pretty soon, even thinking about cats makes you shaky, nervous, and sweaty, with "butterflies" in your stomach. When these things start happening, your fear is no longer helping you to survive danger. Instead, it is using up much of your energy. It is interfering with your enjoyment of life and preventing you from growing up normally. Your fear has become a phobia.

It's unreasonable to be so afraid of cats, but your fear is beyond reason. You can't just say, "Pooh, pooh, I'm not going to be afraid anymore." You need help to overcome your phobia.

Scientists have found that because fears are learned, they can also be unlearned. This means teaching your body to relax, instead of tensing up, whenever you are afraid. You teach your body to behave *as if it were not afraid*. Gradually, your body starts to influence your mind. You start wondering what you were so afraid of in the first place.

In time, by trying hard, you find yourself worrying less about cats, about tests, about playing poorly in an important game, about making friends with someone you really like. Because you are relaxed, chances are you will do much better at tests and games than you ever thought possible. You will become more confident of yourself, and with confidence your fears will be overcome. You may also learn what started your fearful reaction.

But before we discuss how fears develop, let's find out what you really are afraid of.

IDENTIFYING YOUR FEARS

You may already know what situations frighten you. But often fears overlap, or one fear leads to another. It is important to know precisely when and under what circumstances you get anxious and upset.

To do this, we have prepared a self-report form. Take time to copy the list on a separate sheet and then check the situations that make you afraid. Think about each item carefully and try to allow your real feelings to surface. If you have a phobia, your body will often tell you, with sweating, a knotted stomach or a racing heartbeat. Try to imagine that you are really experiencing each of the situations listed. This will help you decide how important your fear is. Only check off things that bother you a lot, and that you spend a lot of time thinking about.

FEAR INVENTORY

1. High places
2. Being shut up in a small space
3. Animals
4. Night or darkness
5. Aircraft
6. Lightning and thunder
7. Insects

8. Nightmares
9. Needles
10. Tests
11. Adults
12. Water
13. Being alone
14. Fire
15. Meeting people
16. Criticism (others getting angry when you make a mistake)
17. Getting hurt
18. Dying
19. Losing valuables
20. Losing your parents
21. Losing your friends
22. Ghosts
23. Scary movies
24. Reading or acting in front of others
25. Doctors and dentists

Perhaps, like Linus in the cartoon on page 11, you are afraid of everything. However, chances are that you have identified one or two or more fears that worry you more than others. We have chosen some of the most common adolescent fears, but there are others—more than 200 of them. So if you know of something else that frightens you, jot it down too, to use in the exercises to follow.

AVOIDANCE

One way to find out what makes you afraid is to try and figure out what you are avoiding. Greg, at fourteen, was a good example of an avoider. He was so

afraid of not making his class sports team in school that he decided not to try out at all.

Although Greg had been quite good at sports for three years, he was afraid the competition in school would be too tough. He kept thinking, over and over: "What will my father say if I fail? What will my friends think? Will they all laugh at me? Who will be my friend? If I did make the team, they probably wouldn't let me play."

By not even trying to make the team, Greg was avoiding the possibility of failure. Avoidance is not very productive, because if you keep avoiding things you'll never know if you can do them or not.

To avoid any possibility of failure in the future Greg would never try anything new. His successes would be very limited, and he would not learn from failure. We all fail at some things during our lifetimes. When we do, it's important to learn from our mistakes so that we will do better in the future.

Avoiding your fears by not facing up to them and not trying may give you temporary relief, but the fears will usually come back to haunt you. Getting rid of fears by avoiding them is like cheating on a test and not getting caught. A student who has done this begins cheating on other tests. Pretty soon he or she is afraid to take a test without hidden notes. The cheater may not get caught on the first few attempts and may start to feel secure. But eventually, cheaters are caught and receive failing grades for cheating. This can also lead to feeling bad about oneself.

Using avoidance to resolve your fears won't help

you to get rid of fear permanently so that it will not bother you in the future. You are simply cheating yourself. But working out what you are avoiding is a good way of finding out what you really fear. If you find yourself avoiding certain things, this is a good indication that fear is motivating your actions. Some examples of avoidance and the fear they indicate are:

Avoiding walking near
lawns where dogs are playing⟶Fear of dogs
Avoiding school by being
sick on the day of a test⟶Fear of failure
Avoiding physical education
class ⟶Fear of competing
Avoiding showing emotion   Fear of strong
to members of your family⟶feelings
Avoiding school dances⟶Fear of rejection
Avoiding giving speeches   Fear of being
in class⟶judged or ridiculed

AVOIDANCE EXERCISE

Take a piece of paper and make a list of three things you tend to avoid. Write each statement as we have above, and put a small arrow toward the fear you are really trying to cover up. Many times you will find more than one fear connected with avoidance actions. For example, avoidance of school may stem from: fear of teachers, fear of competition, fear of rejection, fear of speaking in front of a group, fear of taking tests, fear of being away from home and parents, etc.

13

WHAT FEAR DOES TO YOUR BODY

The next step in learning to control fear is to find out how severe your fears are. You can judge this by noting what fear does to your body. Below is a list of body feelings you may have when you are afraid. Many of these sensations can make you ill if they are allowed to continue for many months and years. By overcoming your fears and phobias now, you will be healthier and much less likely to develop ulcers, high blood pressure and other symptoms that appear when your body experiences a lot of emotional stress. Also, your muscles and stomach will feel a lot less tense.

FEAR INTENSITY PROFILE

Copy the following list and place a check mark next to each of the feelings you have when thinking about or experiencing a fearful situation. If you have identified more than one fear or phobia in the previous fear inventory, work through each one separately.

REACTION

1. Cold chills
2. Sweaty hands
3. Dry mouth
4. Upset stomach
5. Thumping heartbeat
6. Squeaky voice
7. Stuttering or difficulty talking

8. Feel like running away, but can't
9. Face feels hot
10. Hands shake
11. Knees feel weak and shaky
12. Shortness of breath
13. Blurry vision
14. Need to go to the toilet
15. Burping
16. Gassiness
17. Light-headed or dizzy feeling
18. Cold feet
19. Sweaty feet
20. Headache

Now add all the check marks for each fear. Score each phobia as follows: Mild, 1–7; Moderate, 8–14; Severe, 14–20.

RELAXATION

Now that you have a pretty good idea of what makes you afraid and what fear does to your body, you can learn how to overcome these physical effects of fear. You have to teach your body how to relax instead of becoming fearful. This will take some time and will require a lot of practice.

When you are tense and fearful, the muscles in your neck, jaw and scalp tend to contract. Put your fingers on the back of your neck and feel if the muscles are tight. Try to relax them. Sitting comfortably, with both feet on the ground, close your eyes, breathe in deeply and say to yourself, "I am," as you breathe in. Hold for five seconds. As you breathe out say to yourself, "relaxed." Repeat this exercise five times.

You will probably feel a little calmer and less tense. Letting the tension flow out of your muscles is the first step in learning how to relax. Don't worry if you can't feel anything yet. You will have plenty of time for improvement as you follow the exercises throughout the book. We have also provided several relaxation exercises at the end of the book for you to do each day. Learning to relax is like learning to ride a bicycle. At first it takes a lot of effort, but once you've learned, it's easy.

PAIRING FEAR WITH RELAXATION

Once you have learned how to relax completely (and it will take you several weeks to do so), you can go on to the third step in overcoming fears. This is to imagine your fears with the help of a "fear ladder," a list of imaginary situations which helps you relive the fearful experience and "climb out" of your phobia. While you are imagining your fears, you instruct your body to relax. Gradually, you *unlearn* your fears. You teach your body to relax instead of being fearful. As we said before, once you are free of fears, you can live a much happier and more productive life.

In the next chapter we will take a look at some children who have learned to overcome their fears. Even though you may not experience the specific fears mentioned in each chapter, read it anyway. We have included many useful exercises for you throughout the book—each one a little more difficult than the previous one. If the particular fear we talk about doesn't apply to you, just use the exercises to overcome a fear you *do* have.

2
Will I Be Sick for School Today?

School phobias cause most of the problems for children and adolescents, so we will discuss them first.

Just about everyone is afraid of school at one time or another. Generally a school phobia develops because you feel insecure in a new and frightening situation. If you are starting in a new school, you don't have any friends and probably fear you won't make any. Your parents may increase your sense of insecurity by expressing their own worries about how well you will get along with the other kids, and whether you will get good grades. That's the last thing you need. What you really need is reassurance.

You may worry about leaving your mother at home, especially if she is a very worried and anxious person. In fact, she may be more afraid of losing your companionship than you are of leaving home. So she may cling to you for support and make it more difficult for you to face up to your own fears. Perhaps you are secretly angry at her and hope that some harm will come to her. But instead of admitting your anger to yourself, you become afraid that something dreadful will happen to her while you are at school.

So you develop a phobia about going to school, in case she may fall ill or die while you are away. You have suppressed your anger and it has popped up as fear, to prevent you from acknowledging anger. Emotions are funny things—they can't be ignored or wished away. They always come back to haunt you.

Sometimes a phobia will develop to counterbalance changes in your family life. For example, when Greg was twelve, his mother fell ill and his older brother went away to college. Everyone else in the family had to rally round and help. Their family roles changed, and any kind of change causes anxiety.

Instead of allowing himself to admit how anxious he felt about all these changes, Greg focused his anxiety on school and developed a school phobia. In this way, he could pretend that nothing else was bothering him. His phobia may have helped him stay calm away from school, but it didn't do much for his academic work, and he fell far behind in his studies.

As we said, any kind of change is scary. John remembers the day his parents enrolled him in a new school in a town they had just moved to. He was twelve years old. Teachers he had never met before, strange kids and a completely new school made him very scared. He stood in the lunch line not knowing what the prices for the food were and wondering if he had enough money. He was so scared that his legs shook and he began to feel dizzy. He knew that if he didn't sit down soon, he would surely be sick to his stomach.

Fortunately, an understanding teacher saw him in line and took him to the nurse's office. After lying down for a few minutes, he felt much better. The teacher spent some time talking to him about his feelings and told him that he should not be embarrassed. It's quite normal to feel anxious and nervous for the first few days in a new school.

That teacher turned out to be a true friend during John's years at school. She was a very important person in helping him overcome many of his fears. He can still remember her saying that a kid who is afraid of school may try to cover it up by, (1) becoming a troublemaker to get everyone's attention, (2) getting sick and trying to stay home as much as possible, (3) making many trips to the school nurse's office, (4) skipping classes, (5) thinking up new and ingenious ways of getting out of school.

Debbie, fourteen, was always thinking up ways to get out of school. She was sick a great deal and would scream, kick, fight and eventually vomit at the thought of going to school. On weekends she was fine.

Whenever she did manage to get to school she was terribly quiet and shy and had no friends. Most of her friends were either younger children where she lived or her cousins. Although she was bright and had a pleasant personality, she did not feel good about herself and gave herself little credit for the things she did well.

Debbie spent so much time away from school that her grades suffered. A teacher was assigned to work with her at home, but eventually Debbie knew she would have to go back to school, and she was terrified.

Part of the problem was that Debbie had attended eight schools in eight years, because her father's job required the family to move a lot. The only time she had enjoyed school was when her cousin went to the same school. But then Debbie had to move again to a new school. Her attendance record was so bad there that she was suspended from school.

After the Christmas holidays, her new school agreed to let her come back if she promised to attend regularly and to catch up on the work she had missed. On the first day back, some of the other children yelled out to her: "What are you doing back in school? We thought you were retarded." Needless to say, this made Debbie feel terrible. But she gritted her teeth and kept on going.

After nine days of perfect attendance, she convinced the school nurse that she had a very bad stomachache and was sent home for the rest of the day. Five days later, she still had not returned to school. At this point, Debbie needed outside help. Sometimes working on your own is not enough.

If your fear is not too deep-seated and you have not had it for too long, you will find that you can overcome most problems on your own, by using the exercises in this book. And the sooner you start, the better!

In Debbie's case, relaxation exercises were helpful once she got back to school, but the difficult part was getting her inside the classroom. The therapist working with Debbie asked her to sign an attendance contract. This stated that for the first week Debbie promised to stay in school for at least an hour each day. In the following week she was to stay in school two hours, and so on, for seven weeks, until she could stay in school all day.

To make things a little easier, the therapist picked Debbie up each morning, so there would be no fights between Debbie and her parents. They had tried bribes, threats, slappings, spankings, and ignoring her. Nothing worked.

On the first day, Debbie cried a lot and threatened to vomit. But the therapist was firm, and eventually Debbie gave in. She was given permission to come in a little late if necessary. So for the first week they started the day with a scenic tour of the city, to give Debbie time to calm down and think about something pleasant.

For the first few days the therapist stayed in class with Debbie. After they had been in school for the allotted time, they would head for the ice-cream shop to talk over the events of the day.

During this time, Debbie was also given exercises to help her relax and to build her self-confidence. She needed help to become more outgoing with other children and to make friends (see following chapter). Gradually, as she began making friends, she became more courageous about joining in discussions and reading aloud in class.

By the end of seven weeks, Debbie was able to stay in class all day long, and at the end of the school year she had a perfect attendance record.

Debbie's case is typical of many adolescents who develop a school phobia. Does this sound like you? You do better-than-average work, but you tend to isolate yourself from classmates and get little pleasure from your accomplishments. You fear that others will discover your weaknesses and are acutely embarrassed by any mistake or mishap. If you are permitted to remain away from school, you are relaxed and happy, busying yourself with many projects, including your studies, and even cheerfully helping your mother around the house.

But the longer you delay going back to school, the harder it becomes to give up your present life at home for one where you may feel lonely or unsure. Every day you stay away you fall further behind in your studies. So, after a while, your lack of knowledge gives you another reason for fear—the fear that you will embarrass yourself in front of your classmates.

If even the thought of school scares you, try the exercise below and see if it helps you overcome some of that fear. Once you can get your body under control, you can make decisions about what is going to happen to you and what you can do about it. Remember: *Making decisions while you are scared leads to bad decisions.*

Although it is hard to change a pattern once it is firmly established, you can do it if you keep trying. To help you get over your fears, no matter what they are, we will start with simple exercises and progress to more difficult ones. *Do them all.* Success in doing the simpler ones will make it easier to do the harder ones. You may find that some appeal to you more

than others and are easier for you to do. That's OK.
But give every exercise a chance before you discard it.
Wait until you have found the combination of exercises that works for you before you decide that the method isn't any good. Start with the following exercise to help you overcome school phobias:

SCHOOL PHOBIA EXERCISE

1. Imagine something to do with school that scares you. An example might be giving a speech in class or taking a test. Picture the example very clearly in your mind. Try to see yourself in this picture and see how you are reacting. Close your eyes. Pretend that your mind is a television set and that you are playing a movie of your fearful situation on that television. If your fear is about tests, imagine yourself sitting down in the classroom and being handed the test. Picture yourself taking the test, trying to feel the reactions you would have while doing it.

2. Once you have a clear picture, keep your eyes closed and try to feel how your body is reacting. Is your stomach nervous? Do you have a headache? Is your mouth dry? If any of these things are happening to you, then you are duplicating the fear situation.

3. Now, picture yourself in that fearful situation, beginning to relax. Breathe in deeply. Say to yourself, "I am." Breathe out. Say to yourself, "relaxed." Feel the relaxation moving over your

body. As it does, you are beginning to wash away the scared feelings, and you are smiling.

4. Picture yourself finishing the test, giving the speech, participating in the debate or any other type of school activity which might make you nervous. When you use your imagination, you should always imagine that you are *successful* in whatever you are attempting. Be careful: *imagining failure may actually lead to failure.* The more pessimistic your thoughts, the more likely you are to act in a way that will bring about the thing you fear the most.

5. Run your imaginary movie in your head anytime you feel anxiety creeping up on you.

6. The final step involves "acting" in the movie you have created in your head. Some people even write this out, step by step, like a script for a movie, and follow it. Once you have done this several times, it will be easy for you to imagine yourself not being scared and you will be able to put your imaginary self into action in real life.

SPORTS AND TESTS

Patrick, age fifteen, tried another technique to help him overcome his fear of speaking in class. Each time he tried to give a report or answer a question he would stutter so badly no one could understand him. The other students would giggle and laugh at him, and this would make him feel even worse.

He had started stuttering a few years before,

25

when his father first came to watch him play football. Whenever he made a mistake his father would scowl, and after the game, when Patrick tried to explain, his father would say impatiently: "Can't you talk any faster? I don't have all day to wait here and listen to you trying to get out a couple of words."

Of course, the harder Patrick tried, the more he stuttered. This would frustrate his father. Often he would leave the room, throwing up his hands in despair, and saying something like: "That's just great—my only son and he can't even say a sentence straight!"

Pretty soon the stuttering spread to all situations in which adults were present. Now the teacher, principal, football coach, as well as his father, all made him frightened of failing and of being criticized.

To help Patrick overcome his stuttering, his father had to be made to understand that he was too demanding of his son. He expected perfection and criticized Patrick for his failures, instead of praising the boy for his accomplishments and accepting his mistakes. When the therapist explained this to him, Patrick's father learned to deal with his son's difficulties in different ways. He stopped criticizing Patrick so much and became less exasperated by his stuttering.

Patrick started to do the following relaxation exercise to overcome his fears. Soon the stuttering at home and at school diminished, and as it did, he became more confident. His fear of giving speeches in front of the class lessened. Gradually, he learned to replace an anxious, stuttering attitude with a relaxed, confident one. His whole life began to change, and he felt a lot happier than he had before.

Before you get up in front of the class to give a speech, or before taking part in a sports event, you probably feel very tense and nervous. Remember: *Your feelings are nothing more than an exaggeration of the fear response.* Read the following exercises and try to practice them whenever you feel fear coming on:

STUTTERING EXERCISE

1. Take a deep breath. As you breathe in deeply and calmly, repeat to yourself, "My thoughts are calm and clear." Do this five times. You will begin to feel more relaxed.

2. Now imagine yourself reading a favorite book, riding a bicycle, or just goofing around with friends. Allow yourself to imagine doing something you really enjoy. While you are relaxing and enjoying your favorite activity in your mind, you will not be experiencing fearful sensations.

3. Don't try to fight panic or fear. That will only make it worse. Keep relaxing. Each time you feel fear rising, just repeat to yourself slowly, "My thoughts are calm and clear." Breathe deeply several times.

4. Do not run away. If you are in the playground, find a bench to sit on, or lean against a wall or a tree. Don't turn and run home to hide in your bedroom. That's the worst thing you can do.

5. Don't let your imagination run wild with thoughts like: "I just know I'll be sick. I can't help it. I can't control anything." All these thoughts are self-defeating and make your fear grow. *Think positive.*

6. Think about what is really happening to you at this very moment, not just in your thoughts. Ask yourself what the real cause of your fear might be. If you know what you're really afraid of, then you can overcome it.

In thirteen-year-old Michael's case it was easy to work out why he was scared of school. One day while he was eating lunch in the school cafeteria, three older boys came up and started harassing him. They spilled his milk and told him to lick it up off the floor. If he refused, they threatened to beat him up after school. Luckily, a cafeteria monitor saw what was going on and came to his rescue. But before the three boys left, they threatened to get back at Michael later in the day.

Michael was extremely scared and spent the rest of the day wondering if the boys would beat him up after school. By the last period his fear was so great that he left early and went home. He told his mother school had let out early and spent the rest of the afternoon in his room, anxiously looking out the window. He expected to see the three bullies coming up his driveway at any moment.

That evening Michael did not eat much dinner and was very nervous and restless. He had difficulty falling asleep, thinking constantly about the frightening incident. He was sure the boys were going to wait for him at school the next day and beat him up. Even worse, he was frightened of being humiliated in front of all his friends in the cafeteria. Never in his life had he been so scared.

The next morning he faked illness to avoid going to school. The plan worked, and he stayed home all day. But by the end of the day, his anxiety started increasing as he thought about the next day at school. Again the following day, he faked being sick and stayed home.

PRACTICAL STEPS TO TAKE:

Although it was quite normal for Michael to be afraid of school in this case, by staying at home he was running the risk of developing a real phobia. His fear had outlived its usefulness and now threatened to disrupt his life. In order to make himself feel more secure there were several things he could have done. He could have, (1) told his parents or teacher about the incident, (2) asked some of his friends to stick with him for a few days until he felt safer, (3) tried to relax instead of being fearful and anticipating disaster, (4) boosted his self-confidence about handling problems.

Unless you learn to handle your fears reasonably well, you will go through life being intimidated by people and situations that you think you can't handle. The sooner you learn to master your fears, the happier your life will be.

Sick by Shel Silverstein, "Where the Sidewalk Ends"

> "I cannot go to school today."
> Said little Peggy Ann McKay.
> "I have the measles and the mumps,
> A gash, a rash and purple bumps.

My mouth is wet, my throat is dry.
I'm going blind in my right eye.
My tonsils are as big as rocks,
I've counted sixteen chicken pox
And there's one more—that's seventeen,
And don't you think my face looks green?
My leg is cut, my eyes are blue—
It might be instamatic flu.
I cough and sneeze and gasp and choke,
I'm sure that my left leg is broke—
My hip hurts when I move my chin,
My belly button's caving in,
My back is wrenched, my ankle's sprained,
My 'pendix pains each time it rains.
My nose is cold, my toes are numb,
I have a sliver in my thumb.
My neck is stiff, my spine is weak,
I hardly whisper when I speak.
My tongue is filling up my mouth,
I think my hair is falling out.
My elbow's bent, my spine ain't straight,
My temperature is one-o-eight.
My brain is shrunk, I cannot hear,
There is a hole inside my ear.
I have a hangnail, and my heart is—what?
What's that? What's that you say?
You say today is . . . Saturday?
G'bye, I'm going out to play!"

3
Fear of Not Making Friends

It takes self-confidence to face up to fears and to face new challenges and changes in your life. One of the best ways to boost your own confidence is to build up a network of friends whom you like and whom you can trust with your innermost thoughts and fears.

Fears can't be bottled up. By sharing them with someone else, you somehow relieve the tension, like uncapping a bottle of fizzy soda that has been shaken up. If there is no release, it may explode.

You have to learn to like yourself before you can have friends. It's a self-perpetuating cycle. If you don't like yourself, others will not like you. Then you will like yourself even less, because you have no friends.

At the age of twelve, Tom had that problem. He was too frightened to mix with other children in the playground, and so, was never asked to join in their games. In sports class he was always the last person to be chosen for a team because he was not very good at most of the games and was afraid of making a mistake.

His fear had started in the first grade, when he was one of the smallest boys in the class and was always picked last. But now that he had grown to be as tall as everyone else, he was still scared. Instead of taking the risk and trying to develop some skill in sports, he stopped trying. He got his parents to write a letter to the school asking that he be excused from sports altogether.

Tom became known as a loner and no one asked him to participate in any activities. He was a very sad and lonely boy, whose fear of making friends and of trying anything new was growing worse all the time. Gradually he developed a phobia about making friends and became very depressed. Tom had to learn to like himself and to boost his self-confidence before he could make new friends.

If you feel a bit like Tom and want to learn to like yourself better, try this:

PLAN FOR LEARNING TO LIKE YOURSELF

1. Find a mirror. Try to find one large enough to reflect your head and shoulders clearly.

2. Stand there and look at yourself. Think about how you would describe yourself to someone else.

3. Make a list of all the things you like about the way you look. Start with the superficial things first, because right or wrong, people first judge you by your appearance. So the first thing you have to learn in building self-confidence is to like the way you look, and if you don't, do something about it. (We will talk about some of the things you do well later, because in the

long run these are the most important things about you. But it's hard even to get to first base if no one wants to talk to you.)

4. Now think of someone you admire—perhaps a movie star, a football player, a teacher, somebody's older brother or sister. Choose someone who looks a bit like you. Don't try to model yourself after someone who looks completely unlike you—you might get depressed because you can never possibly look like that person.

5. Find a picture of your hero or heroine, if you can. Analyze how they look. Do you resemble them? Do you have the same hair or the same mouth? Is there some way you could improve your own looks, perhaps by cutting your hair, or letting it grow longer? If there is something you know you can do to make yourself look better, then do it. There's nothing wrong with trying to look as good as you possibly can. It makes you feel good inside. Perhaps you're secretly afraid that if you do try harder to look good and people *still* don't like you, then you're really sunk. Don't worry. Just take one step at a time.

Try to find as many similarities as you can between yourself and the person you admire. Notice that your hero or heroine is not perfect either. Trying to be perfect can leave you discouraged and feeling bad about yourself. Pretty soon you will begin to realize that the way you look is perfectly OK. No one way of looking is better than any other. No matter what you look like, you can find somebody you admire whom you also resemble.

Of course, nobody likes a conceited, vain person either. So don't get carried away about how handsome or pretty you are. Just remember you are as handsome or as pretty as you feel. Others will accept you as handsome or pretty if you think of yourself that way.

Now, let's concentrate on some of the more important things—things going on inside your head that make you unique and different and lovable in your own special way. Make a list of the things you do well, such as playing the piano or guitar, writing poems or stories, painting, building models, collecting stamps, anything you enjoy and feel good about doing.

Be aware that good looks and beauty, no matter how important they may seem, are not the most important things in life. Chances are, some of the most popular kids in your school are not popular simply because they have straight teeth, a clear complexion and wear nice clothes. They also believe in themselves and *do* things that make them feel good, like playing football, running for election to the school council or playing in the school orchestra.

Notice, too, that when you are busily involved in your favorite occupation or hobby you forget about what other people think of you. You are enjoying yourself too much to care. And your hobby can help you meet people with whom you have a common interest, not just superficially, but something you are both good at, can talk about, and spend time doing together. This is how firm, close friendships are built— through mutual sharing, exploring feelings and ideas, and spending time together. It takes time, but it's well worth the trouble.

If you are timid and shy, don't be afraid to admit your fear of making friends to your parents or your teachers. They may be able to help. Discuss your problem with a sister or brother or some of the kids at school. If anyone laughs at you, you can be quite sure that they are even more afraid of making friends than you are. People who laugh at other people's fears usually have the same fears themselves, only they refuse to admit it.

PRETENDING TO BE FEARLESS

Richard, who was fifteen, was the kind of kid who made fun of other children for being "chicken" or a "scaredy-cat." For as long as anyone could remember, he had been the class show-off and the most daring kid in school. In the early grades, he would start by showing off and, if this did not get him the attention he wanted, he would begin daring the other students to follow him in dangerous stunts. If anybody refused, Richard would yell out: "What are you, some kind of chicken? You're probably afraid of your own shadow. Anybody who is scared doesn't have guts." Most of the kids thought that Richard was the bravest student in the whole school. He wanted everyone to think of him as a person who had no fears.

When the therapist first met Richard and talked with him, he noticed that almost every time Richard said something, it was to show off his bravery. The therapist soon learned what Richard was really trying to say.

Before Richard became the "fearless boy," he had

not been doing well in school and was not very well liked by his classmates. He did not participate in sports and kept to himself. He was deeply hurt when the other students made fun of him, and his father was always pushing him to do better at everything.

At night, Richard's father would ask him: "Why can't you join the football team? You can get better grades, if you really try. Why can't you be like the rest of the kids?" Every time his father said these things, they hurt Richard deeply, but he had learned not to let anyone know when he was hurt. Instead he decided to pretend to be fearless.

This happened quite by accident. One day, after school, several boys were walking along the top of a seven foot block wall. They challenged Richard to come up on the wall with them. They were sure he never would. Richard had been kidded enough and so he climbed onto the wall. His legs were shaking so badly he thought he would fall. At the end of the wall he slipped, and while trying to regain his balance he had to stand on one leg. He regained his balance, but to his surprise all the boys were now cheering him, not taunting him anymore. They thought he had performed the one-legged trick on purpose. From then on, Richard knew how to make friends and impress the other kids.

After talking with the therapist several times, Richard admitted that he was very scared when he performed some of his daring stunts, but he kept on doing them because he was afraid of not having friends. Once he admitted having fears, the psychologist could give him advice on how to change his actions and be happier.

Richard's real fears, underlying his showing off, were, (1) fear of not getting approval from his parents, especially his father, (2) fear that his friends would not like him, (3) fear that he would not have any friends, (4) fear that he was not a worthwhile person.

Once Richard understood his fears and was willing to talk about them, he was able to learn how to control them. The fears no longer controlled him. He was ready to make friends without being a show-off. Richard went through an assertiveness scheme to help him make friends. You can do it too.

MAKING FRIENDS EXERCISE

1. You must develop a plan to deal with the situation before it occurs. Don't just sit there and become anxious, because worrying won't help solve the problem. Think about what you have to do to make a new friend and plan how you are going to act. You may want to ask your friends or your parents for help with your plan. Making a plan keeps you thinking positively and helps get rid of worries.

2. Rehearse your first meeting with someone by writing out all the steps you will follow.

    (a) There is a new student in your class and you would like to meet him.

(b) After school, as you are walking from class, you see the new student walking toward you.

(c) You smile and he smiles back.

(d) You feel your heart begin to beat faster as he gets closer.

(e) You wonder if you'll know what to say.

(f) He is less than ten feet away and you know you'll have to say something to him.

(g) The person comes up to you and stops.

(h) You say, "Hi" and ask him how he likes the new school.

(i) The new student answers your question and you begin talking.

(j) You both walk toward your next class.

3. Stand in front of a mirror and repeat out loud what you will say. Tell yourself that you can meet the challenge and handle the situation. Think about a positive outcome to the meeting. Then try to relax just before you meet the person. When you feel fear coming on, breathe in deeply, and as you exhale, silently say the word "relax" to yourself.

4. After you have talked with the person and found your method does work, don't hesitate to pat yourself on the back and feel good about it. While you were talking, you may still have felt some nervousness. You can't change your reactions overnight. But each time you talk to someone new successfully, your fear will become less and less. You will soon realize that what you

feared was much worse than what really happened. Congratulate yourself, and realize that each time you use these assertive procedures to overcome a fear, you are making progress.

Say to yourself, *"I did it!"*

FEAR OF DATING

Susie, age thirteen, was in the seventh grade. Most of her friends were interested in boys, but Susie was scared of them. Some of her friends had gone out on dates, but Susie was even afraid to talk to boys. Anytime a boy came near her, she would make an excuse to get away as soon as possible. The boys, realizing she was frightened, began to tease her. The more they teased, the more afraid she became. If a boy so much as bumped into her in the hallway, it was enough to make her feel sick to her stomach.

What was Susie really afraid of? She was scared of all the changes that come with growing up. Her body was starting to change. She was becoming more like a woman and less like a child. She was frightened of losing her parents' love and having to find other people to love.

Growing up also means taking on more responsibility. As a child, you are taken care of by your parents. As you get older, they expect you to do a few chores around the house. In return, they give you more freedom, letting you go out by yourself to visit friends or stay out a little later in the evening. For every step you take away from your parents, you are expected to be more independent and more responsible. If you make a mistake, no one is going to cover up for you, or provide excuses. You are responsible for your own actions. This can be frightening.

Because you are no longer a child but not yet an adult, you are probably anxious about how to behave. You have doubts about whether you will succeed in your ambitions, and you worry about being successful. All this worry and fear can lead to shyness, sensitivity and angry outbursts at your parents. You are unclear about your role in life, and you want someone to show you the way, yet you don't want anyone telling you what to do.

Between the ages of ten and fourteen, it is natural to feel some anxiety about growing up. The thought of having a friendship with another boy or girl may be frightening. These are things you have to work out as you get older. They are natural fears, not phobias, but you can use help to overcome them.

Around the same time that girls are finding out how to be women and how to be attractive to boys, the boys are having their own problems. Even today, despite changes in the way we think about the way men and women should behave, boys are still expected to be tough and not to need comforting. Many boys feel ashamed of crying even if they are lonely or ill-treated. They feel they have to be brave even when they are badly frightened. If boys are not as courageous as they are expected to be, some people consider them "unmanly" or weak.

Fortunately, parents are beginning to realize how important it is that you be allowed to express your fears. Having a fear and never talking about it to anybody, or not even wanting to think about it yourself, can make you feel as if you are going to explode. Well, you're not going to explode; but if you keep these fears inside and do not try to solve them, the emotional explosions that happen inside you can leave you feeling sad, depressed, angry, and frustrated.

ADMIT YOUR FEARS

Take a moment to stand in front of a mirror again and finish this sentence: "I am scared of. . . ."

If you can admit to yourself that you are scared of certain things, you have a much better chance of learning to control your fears. You may find that as you grow up, other things will frighten you, but you will know how to deal with them so they won't grow out of proportion and paralyze you.

Many kids say things like this: I'm too ashamed to talk about my fears. Everyone would laugh at me if they knew I was scared. It's better to keep those kinds of things inside. All the guys on the team would laugh at me if they knew. I would be the laughing stock of the school if they knew. Talking about it won't do any good. If I tell my parents, they'll send me to a psychiatrist.

Every one of the above statements has been repeated over and over by people your age who are afraid to talk about their fears. Worse still, they are afraid even to admit they are scared.

Don't imagine that after reading this book you will never be scared again. Of course you will. But you won't be afraid to admit it any longer. Gradually you will learn new ways of building up your confidence, and pretty soon you will feel brave enough to handle new challenges as they arise.

4
Fear of Doctors, Dentists, and Hospitals

Any perfectly healthy person who develops an over-whelming fear of illness, such as cancer, has an illness phobia. It is more than just hypochondria, in which you are generally anxious and worry over every little ache and pain.

Illness phobia sometimes develops because by concentrating on your fear of illness you can avoid thinking about other things that bother you, such as an unhappy home life, lack of friends or problems in school. Doctors also notice that a great deal of publicity about certain illnesses increases people's fears. Right after Betty Ford and Happy Rockefeller had operations for breast cancer, there was a huge increase in the number of frightened women coming in for cancer checkups. Of course, in a way, this was good, because the earlier cancer is detected, the greater the chance of survival. But unfortunately, concentrating on sickness rather than on health seems to weaken your resistance to disease. You are more likely to fall sick if you think about it a great deal. This is a clear example of how fearing the worst can actually make it happen.

Going to the doctor or dentist can be scary sometimes. And your fear mushrooms because you anticipate the worst. If you only see doctors and dentists when you feel sick or are in pain, you will naturally come to think of medical or dental care as a painful, frightening experience. It's quite normal to fear the unknown when you don't know what's wrong with you or what the doctor or dentist will do. But if you need medical or dental care, your fear may interfere with getting adequate care.

Many adults are afraid of doctors, too. Even some doctors are afraid to visit other doctors. So don't be ashamed of your fear. Simply learn better ways to handle your emotions. Sitting in the doctor's office feeling terrified, or fainting at the sight of a needle will not help you, and it may actually make the treatment more painful because you exaggerate the experience in your mind.

FEAR OF DOCTORS

Cindy, twelve, was so scared of doctors that even the thought of getting an injection would throw her into a temper tantrum and she would insist to anyone who would listen that she definitely was not going to see the doctor. She would scream, "I don't care if I am sick; I'm not going!" Finally, her parents stopped taking her to the doctor, except for a real emergency.

Cindy's fear was not so much of what was actually being done. She didn't mind the injections and blood tests all that much. Her real fear was of what *might* happen, and this caused her the greatest agony. Cindy watched a lot of television. Every time something happened to people in a show and they had to go to the hospital, she would imagine the same thing happening to herself. She identified with all the people being operated on, all the people with broken legs, and all those who died in the hospital.

Consequently, whenever she knew it was time to see the doctor again, she began having nightmares about horrible things happening to her. These nightmares and fearful daydreams would occur more frequently as the day for the doctor's visit approached. Her parents tried to help her by not telling her in advance of a doctor's appointment, hoping that in this way she wouldn't be so scared. But it didn't help, because Cindy's fear of doctors was so firmly implanted.

Part of Cindy's problem was her poor relationship with her parents. Instead of encouraging Cindy to express her emotions, they believed "children should be seen and not heard." Because of Cindy's problem, the whole family eventually went for counseling. The doctor advised Cindy's parents to allow their daughter more freedom in expressing her anger and frustration. He also asked them to be more tolerant of her natural feelings of anxiety as she grew older and faced new challenges.

Sometimes parents who are extremely insecure themselves, and who feel inadequate about being parents, find it very hard to tolerate anxiety in their children. They want their children to be strong and fearless because they themselves feel weak. Any anxiety in their children makes them feel nervous and guilty that they are not doing a good job as parents. In a way, they are asking their children to be stronger than they are, in effect, to be their parents. Of course, this is not fair to the child, and the parents have to work on building up their own self-confidence. But in the meantime, children (especially adolescents) have to realize that parents can't always be towers of strength. They, too, have their own fears and worries to work out. Hopefully, though, your parents can provide enough support to make you feel secure most of the time.

RELAXATION EXERCISE

In addition to participating in the family counseling, Cindy learned the following exercise to help her to relax. Once you have read it over carefully and either memorized it or put it on a tape recorder, you should do the exercise for five minutes two or three times a day, with your eyes closed:

1. Imagine you are walking along a beach on a warm, sunny day. Listen to the waves as they roll up against the shore. Feel the salt ocean spray as it touches your face. Notice the sand softly giving way to your feet as you walk along. You find a place to sit and relax, to enjoy the sound of the

ocean and the smell of the salt water. You breathe in contentedly as you relax in this situation.

2. Imagine the word *calm*. Imagine this word as you sit beside the sea. While you keep this in mind, relax the muscles of your toes. Wiggle them, and pretend the warm summer sun is gently beaming down on you as you enjoy yourself.

3. Relax your leg muscles. Allow them to become warm and limp. Relax the muscles of your thighs and the muscles around your face. Think of the pleasant scene and think of the word *calm*.

4. Relax your stomach muscles. Relax the muscles in your back, allowing your back to go limp. Now relax the muscles of your chest. Breathe easily and comfortably.

5. Keep imagining the pleasant scene and relax the muscles in your arms. They feel so good as they relax. Relax the muscles in your forehead and scalp and the muscles between your eyebrows, where you frown. Relax your eyelids. Let them feel heavy.

6. Allow the muscles on the bridge of your nose to become relaxed, also the muscles around your nostrils and your jaw. Your teeth are slightly parted as you become more relaxed. Your jaw is hanging slack as you relax more and more.

7. Keep imagining this pleasant scene and the word *calm*. Check out your body for any tense spots. Take them a spot at a time and let them go. Just

keep allowing yourself, allowing your body, to get calm and relaxed, calm and relaxed, becoming very loose, limp and relaxed.

8. Now count backwards from three to one and at the count of one open your eyes and sit up. "Three, two, one. Hello, world."

You can record this exercise on a tape recorder or have a parent or friend read it to you as you sit comfortably in a chair. You should do this exercise three times a day for five minutes until your body feels completely relaxed. Set a time for doing it and stick to it—when you get up, after lunch or before you go to bed, for example.

After Cindy had learned how to relax, the therapist helped her write out the following fear ladder. Each scene was written on a separate card, which helped Cindy visualize her fear.

FEAR LADDER FOR PHYSICAL EXAMINATION

1. Your parents tell you it is time for a physical examination.
2. You are in your parents' car on the way to the doctor's office.
3. You are waiting in the lobby, trying to keep your mind off what is going to happen.
4. The nurse calls your name and it is time to go into the examining room, where you wait for the doctor.

5. The doctor comes in and talks to you before the examination.
6. The doctor begins to examine you.
7. The doctor tells you that you need an injection.
8. The nurse comes in and prepares the injection.
9. You sit there and watch her putting the liquid into the syringe.
10. The nurse gives you the injection.

Once Cindy had completed the list, she started to do her relaxation exercises as she thought of each item on the list. The cards were arranged from the least fearful experience to the most fearful. She went slowly, working at two items each day. At one point, she had difficulty relaxing, so she went a little slower until she could successfully go over all ten items while remaining completely relaxed. You can do the same thing on your own. Use one of the fear ladders we have prepared for you, at the back of the book. Pick out one that relates to a fear you have, or make up your own.

UNLEARNING YOUR FEAR

1. Allow yourself to relax using the relaxation method described above, or turn to the back of the book and find the more complete relaxation exercise. Ask someone to tape or read you the exercise. Play the tape for yourself before beginning on the fear ladder.
2. Pick up your fear ladder and picture the first

scene in your mind for ten to twenty seconds while remaining completely relaxed. Let yourself get completely into the picture. Imagine that you are actually in that scene, experiencing the smells, sounds and touches of that scene. Don't be upset if you find this difficult the first several times you try it. After practice, you will be able to imagine yourself in the scene quite clearly. Try not to let outside thoughts interfere.

The more accurately you visualize the scene, the better you will experience exactly how it feels to be there. Try to remain as deeply relaxed as possible while you imagine the scene.

3. After about thirty seconds, stop visualizing the fear ladder scene and imagine yourself in a very familiar and relaxing place. Again, this may be at the beach, or at the movies, watching television, or reading a book, as long as it is something very relaxing and pleasant for you to imagine. You will return to this very pleasant and relaxing place after imagining each one of the scenes on your fear ladder. By imagining the comfortable scene, you will be able to relax your body completely after imagining the fearful scene.

4. Now, repeat the same procedure for the second scene on your fear ladder, imagining the scene vividly for ten to twenty seconds while trying to remain relaxed.

5. Turn off the fear ladder scene and return to the comfortable scene you imagined earlier.

6. That's as far as you will go on the first day. You

should only imagine two new scenes each day. On the second day you will do the process for scenes 1 through 4; on the third day, you will work with scenes 1 through 6, etc. This way, getting through the ten scenes will take you five days. It is most important that you remember to remain relaxed at all times.

The main point of desensitization is to pair relaxation with a situation that normally scares you. Gradually you train your body to stop acting scared and you learn to control your fears.

Cindy found that the next time she was due to go to the doctor, although she still was scared, she could relax enough to go through with the ordeal. Of course, injections do hurt a little bit. But Cindy's fears had been so exaggerated that the injection hurt even more than it need have. She was as tense as a guitar string, so the needle hurt more as it went in. When Cindy learned how to relax, the shots hurt a lot less.

It's quite normal to feel some fear before an operation, or of going into a hospital for any reason. What you need more than anything else is confidence in your doctor and reassurance that everything will turn out fine.

PLAN FOR EASING FEAR OF HOSPITALIZATION

If you do have to go into the hospital for blood tests or an operation, take these practical steps to help lessen your fears:

1. Ask your parents to find out as much as they can about the procedure and tell you about it, or ask the doctor yourself. Most doctors know from experience that their patients hurt less and get well more quickly when they know what to expect. So don't ever be afraid of asking questions. And if you don't understand the long words the doctor uses, ask him to explain them.

2. Talk with another person your age who has been in the hospital for a similar operation. Find out from him or her what it was like. Ask whether you are allowed to take toys, games, or a special bathrobe or nightclothes from home to make you feel more comfortable.

3. Ask to visit the children's ward before you have to go in. Talk to the other patients and nurses there and confide your fears to them. Once all your fears are out in the open and the unknown becomes known, it is not quite so scary.

4. Sometimes doctors will have to take blood samples for tests. Don't be afraid that they will take too much. Although blood is precious and you can't live without it, your body is constantly making new blood. So anytime you lose some blood, the cells in your bone marrow will make more.

5. Ask a nurse if you can hold her hand and squeeze tight if something hurts. And don't be afraid to cry if you feel like it. Crying is the body's way of getting rid of hurtful experiences. If you don't cry, you store up the hurt feelings inside yourself, where they can do more harm. Even if you've

been taught that "only sissies cry," try to remember that crying is nothing to be ashamed of. Sometimes it takes more courage to show your true feelings than to keep them locked up inside.

Over half the people in the United States and Britain don't visit a dentist regularly. For many of them, fear of pain keeps them away. Being afraid of the dentist is a lot like being scared of doctors, so you can practice some of the same exercises. Also, take some practical steps to reassure yourself:

PLAN FOR EASING FEAR OF DENTISTS

1. Ask your parents if you can go along the next time either one of them visits the dentist. Explain to the dentist what you want to do and get his or her permission in advance. Watching someone you know go through an experience that frightens you, helps you overcome your own fear. You gain courage by watching them. You tell yourself: "If they can do it, so can I."
2. Ask the dentist to explain what he or she is going to do before it is done, and to show you the various instruments dentists use.
3. Ask him or her to warn you about unusual noises or sensations which may occur during treatment. Knowing exactly what will happen and how long a procedure will last helps keep your imagination from running wild.

When you are frightened, your mouth often becomes quite dry. Dentists have found the drier your mouth is, the more cavities you develop. Saliva helps wash away the food and bacteria that cause cavities. So try to keep your fear level down through relaxation, and you'll be rewarded with healthier teeth.

To help you get over your fear of dentists, try the following exercise:

FEAR OF DENTIST EXERCISE

1. Turn to the back of the book and find the fear ladder for dentists. Write out each step of the ladder on a separate index card.
2. Take a deep breath and exhale slowly. Now hold your breath by placing one hand over your mouth and pinching your nose. Hold it for as long as you possibly can.
3. As you breathe in again to take a gulp of air, have someone hold up the first card of the fear ladder in front of you, so you can read it clearly.
4. Keep holding your breath and releasing until you no longer feel tension about the situation presented on that card. Now move on to the next card and repeat your breathing exercise.

You will find that the release of tension after holding your breath helps to relieve tension all over your body, and you will not be able to remain afraid for long.

You may have to use this technique twice a day for several weeks before you are completely ready to go to the dentist without panicking. While you are at the dentist, use the relaxation exercise at the back of the book to help you stay calm. As you do the exercises, be careful to avoid hyperventilation—breathing so rapidly that you become dizzy or lightheaded.

5
Animal Fears and Phobias

More people have phobias about animals than about anything else. Repeated parental warnings to "watch out for that dog," or "be careful, the cat may scratch you," can succeed in terrifying you, sometimes so successfully that you never outgrow your fear.

Of course, if you were walking down the street alone and a large dog came up and growled at you, you'd be scared no matter how old you were, and running away might be the most sensible thing to do. In this case your fight-or-flight response helps keep you out of danger. But if a little dog, which poses no threat to you, brings on a fight-or-flight response, your fear has got the best of you.

If your parents are afraid of certain animals, then you are quite likely to develop the same fears. If a mother screams every time she sees a spider, her daughter will learn to scream also, but her son will have learned to cover up his fear and not let it show. Cultural conditioning is a very powerful force, determining what is an acceptable and what is an unacceptable reaction for each sex. How many men, for example, would admit that they are frightened of mice? Many children learn to be brave by imitating a brave parent.

Small children's imaginations can produce all sorts of animal fears. When Freddy, age three, heard his mother complain, "Ants eat everything up," he began to wonder if he could be "eaten up" too. Television fantasies and cartoons can convince young children that anything is possible. You usually outgrow such fears, but sometimes they stay with you, especially if you have had a frightening experience, as Jerry had.

Jerry was thirteen. He joined the school track team and competed in the running jump. During one of the after-school sessions, he was walking along the field when several bees buzzed around his head. He paid no attention to them and went over to the jump pit.

He made a couple of practice jumps.

The third time Jerry jumped, a bee buzzed by his face again and he ducked to one side but was stung painfully on the ear. Jerry was a little frightened, since he had never been stung before.

When he went back to the track the next day, something had changed. Every time a bee or even a fly came near him, Jerry covered his head and ran like mad. Because of the bright flowers in the grass around the playing field there were many bees around, so Jerry ran away. He didn't jump that afternoon, or for the rest of the week. Although his parents and his coach tried to reassure him, Jerry was terrified of bees and nothing could persuade him to go back to the track field. Even in his dreams he imagined bees stinging him, and he stopped going outside if there was the slightest chance that there might be insects flying around.

In the beginning, Jerry's fear was normal. However, the next time he saw a bee he acted as if he had been stung again. His mind was beginning to run wild. He started imagining that all flying insects were out to do him harm. A phobia began to develop, like a snowball rolling down a hill—picking up speed and getting bigger and bigger.

Jerry's phobia changed his life so he, (1) didn't want to go outside during the daytime, (2) left the track team, and (3) felt bad about himself as his friends began to tease him.

Jerry was a timid boy to begin with, and his fear of bees gave him the excuse he had been looking for to quit the track team. He was afraid of losing at an important upcoming meet, and he also hated traveling to the meet with some of the other kids, who were noisy and rowdy.

But quitting is no way to solve a problem. Jerry's fear had now gone beyond the point where he could remember why it started. He needed a simple technique to overcome his fear of insects before he could even begin to think about his shyness and timidity.

FEAR OF INSECTS EXERCISE

1. Jerry was told to clap his hands loudly every time he thought about his fear of bees. This distracted him from thinking about the bees and shifted his attention from his fear to the noise.
2. With practice, he was gradually able to switch from clapping his hands to snapping his fingers. This was a less noticeable activity and he could do it in public without embarrassment.
3. He learned to relax thoroughly by using the relaxation exercise at the end of the book.
4. Finally, by snapping his fingers he could signal his body to relax.

Overcoming his fear of flying insects gave Jerry a feeling of success. He began to realize that he could apply the same techniques to help him overcome his shyness and fear of standing up to bullies. Pretty soon he became a much calmer person with more self-confidence and enjoyed a much happier life.

FEAR OF DOGS

For Mary, age fifteen, it was more difficult to find out why she was scared of dogs. For as long as she could remember, even the smallest dogs terrified her. Her mother no longer knew what to do. The family doctor had suggested consulting a psychologist, but Mary's father had scoffed at the idea, saying that his daughter would get over her fear in time. But time was running out. Mary's fear of dogs prevented her from walking a short distance to school or even playing outside in the afternoon.

Her mother had coaxed her into playing volleyball with several girls near her house one afternoon, and the simple task of getting her out the front door had taken more than twenty minutes.

Mary was embarrassed by her fear of dogs and tried to hide it when she was around her friends. This was becoming increasingly difficult, because there were many dogs where she lived. Although the community required that dogs were to be on a leash, most people allowed their dogs to wander freely.

Mary tried to remember back to a time when she was not afraid of dogs and couldn't do so. Whenever she saw a dog she froze and no matter how hard she tried, her legs would not move. Sometimes she could scream, and this would propel her into activity. She would race back towards her house. Dogs didn't even have to bark to set off this fear reaction.

Some of the kids who knew about her fear were extremely unkind and started calling her "dog-girl" and teasing her with pictures of dogs, threatening to bring them to her house.

The children thought Mary's problem must be a joke. They found it inconceivable that a fifteen-year-old girl could be so frightened of dogs that didn't even bark at her.

Mary began to realize that something was really wrong with her. Her best friend had been bitten on the arm by a German shepherd, but was not afraid of all dogs, only of German shepherds. Other dogs didn't seem to bother her at all.

Mary was confused, her parents were confused, and no one could solve the problem. Mary's grades were suffering, and she was losing her friends. On weekends, she would lie in the house, where she felt safe. Her parents drove her to and from school, so she would have no chance of running into any dogs. But a dog barking in the middle of the night would awaken Mary from a deep sleep and trigger the same reaction as if the dog were standing in front of her.

Mary finally went to see a psychologist on the advice of her family doctor. At first, Mary was frightened, but once she found out that the therapist could be her friend and wanted to help her, she began talking freely.

The psychologist began by trying to find out when Mary's fear had started. She couldn't remember ever having been attacked or bitten by a dog. Eventually, the doctor discovered that an older sister used to take Mary for walks when she was about three. Mary's sister was a dog lover and brought along bits of food for any stray dogs they met along the way.

Because Mary was small for her age, she was dwarfed by even medium-sized dogs. The older girl would call the dogs over and have them jump in the air to get pieces of meat. At first this thrilled Mary, but when one of the dogs crashed into her she became frightened. She wasn't hurt physically, but from that point on, Mary would hide behind her sister whenever dogs were around.

Her sister told her she was foolish—that dogs

were friendly and would not hurt her. Mary could remember the terror that welled up inside her as her sister called over one dog after another.

Often, when it was time for a walk, Mary would say she was sick. When she couldn't find an excuse, she would beg her sister not to let the dogs come near, but her sister didn't take her fear seriously and continued to take along snacks for the dogs.

After a few months, her sister stopped taking Mary for walks. But from then on, Mary's phobia toward dogs grew. Pictures of ferocious dogs on television and news items about wolves or wild dog packs only confirmed her belief that dogs were evil and would attack her if they could.

RELAXATION EXERCISE

Mary learned to relax using this simple method, which you can use, too.

1. Ask yourself, is there any tension in my legs or my thighs? If there is, take it a spot at a time, tense the muscle and then let it go. Even if it feels relaxed, allow yourself to become more relaxed. Allow those muscles to become more loose, limp, and relaxed.
2. Ask yourself, is there any tension in my abdomen? My back or my chest? If there is, take it a spot at a time and first tense these muscles, then let them go, breathing easily and comfortably the way you do in a deep sleep.

3. Ask yourself, is there any tension in my fingers, in my arms, or in my shoulders? If there is, take a spot at a time, tense, and let it go. Try to let them feel pleasantly limp and heavy as the muscles relax. Stop fighting gravity.

4. Ask yourself, is there any tension between my shoulder blades or in my neck? If there is, tense it, then let it go. Your head falls limply back to the chair.

5. Ask yourself, is there any tension in my face, in my jaw, or in my throat? If there is, let that tension go. Let all the tension flow out of your body until you are completely relaxed.

Next, Mary made a list of all the things about dogs that frightened her. If you want to do the exercise, change anything that doesn't seem right for you.

FEAR LADDER FOR DOGS

1. You're walking along the street and you see a dog.
2. You keep walking, and the dog starts to come near you.
3. The dog is now 100 feet away.
4. You stop walking, but the dog is still coming closer to you. It is not barking or acting cross.
5. The dog is about thirty feet away, and you can see it very clearly.
6. The dog looks at you and keeps coming closer.
7. The dog is only five feet away from you, and you keep staring at it.

8. The dog comes up to you and starts to sniff around your legs.
9. You reach down and carefully pat the dog on the top of its head.
10. The dog seems a little scared but licks your hand and begins to follow you as you continue walking.

Different animals, such as a cat, or a specific kind of dog, may be substituted for the dog. Don't worry if you have trouble with any one phase of the fear ladder. The worst thing you can do is try too hard. Just keep relaxing and work your way through the ladder two stages at a time, or more slowly if you find that too difficult.

Once you feel thoroughly confident about your ability to remain relaxed, go out with a friend who is not afraid of dogs and try to act out the exercise in real life. You will be amazed at your own ability to stay calm when a dog approaches you. (Some fear of dogs is perfectly reasonable, however, since dogs really can bite!)

SIGNS OF RELAXATION

How do you know when you are *really* relaxed and ready to face up to your fears in real life? The following body sensations tell you you are relaxed enough to test out your fears:

1. Arms or legs feel heavy
2. Breathing is slow and regular

3. Heartbeat is steady
4. Hands or feet tingle
5. Drowsy feeling
6. Jaw feels heavy
7. Shoulders droop slightly
8. Sounds become distant

Use this list to check your success in relaxing. You should not attempt to face up to your fears in real life until you have been able to go through the fear ladder completely while feeling *at least four* of these signs of relaxation.

6
Fear of Travel

Taking a trip should be fun!

It isn't fun if you are scared to travel in a car, boat, train or aircraft. Fear of traveling is quite understandable, since accidents do happen and are often widely publicized. But it can ruin your vacation and your family's. Dina's story is a good example of this kind of fear.

While waiting in the airport, Dina, age fifteen, went to the ladies' room four times in less than twenty minutes. She told everybody she could not help it, she had to go. Dina's stomach felt as nervous as a mouse in a room full of cats. Her parents had arrived at the airport early this time, just in case. For a previous trip, the doctor had given her some pills to take. He said they would make her sleepy on the aircraft and calm her down. But the pills didn't work. In fact, they made her even more wide-awake. Her older brothers tried to help, but after a little while began to tease her because they didn't want to have their trip ruined.

When her parents said that they might drive to Florida, instead of flying, her brothers became very upset and angry with her.

Dina had always been a little scared of flying, but her fear became much worse after two jets crashed in the Canary Islands and Dina saw pictures of the disaster in a national magazine. These pictures showed injured people, and the planes bursting into flames. Every time she thought about flying, she thought about the pictures. She wasn't even thinking of the good times they would have at Disney World—only her fear that the plane would crash.

Dina's family was sitting in the departure lounge, not talking for fear that would aggravate Dina's problem. The announcement came over the airport loudspeaker that it was time to board the plane. Dina's father got up and turned to hold her hand on the way to the plane, but Dina was nowhere in sight. Her parents walked out into the hallway just in time to see Dina heading into the ladies' room again.

Dina's story is not unusual. Many people are afraid of planes, trains, boats and even cars. Not everyone will have the same reason for being afraid. Some of them are, (1) seeing an accident on television or in the movies, (2) reading about an accident in a newspaper or magazine, (3) being in an accident, (4) being scared by what other people say about traveling, (5) using other people as models—for example, sitting in an aircraft and being very calm until you see that your mother is scared, then becoming scared too, (6) thinking that you are supposed to be scared—for example, believing that girls should be scared of fast cars.

If you are afraid of flying, take a moment to write out this fear ladder on index cards.

FEAR LADDER FOR FLYING

1. You find out that you are going on a trip and you will be flying to your destination.
2. As you enter the airport, planes are landing and taking off. You can hear the noise of their jet engines.
3. Inside the terminal, people are walking around, and you hear announcements of planes taking off and landing.
4. Your parents have the tickets, and you sit waiting for the announcement of your plane.
5. Your flight is announced, and you walk on board the plane, and are greeted by the stewardess. Once in your seat, you look out the window and see the men getting the plane ready for takeoff.
6. The plane begins to move down the runway and you feel the shaking and the loud noise as the pilot increases power.
7. Slowly the plane lifts off the ground and you can feel yourself pressed back into the seat. In a few minutes, the landing gear comes up and you feel and hear a loud thumping.
8. You are very high in the air and you can hear the sounds of the engines and the noise inside the plane.

9. As you get close to your destination, the plane begins to go down to approach for a landing. The ground gets closer and closer. Soon you can see cars, and you notice how tiny they look.
10. The landing gear goes down with a loud thump and the plane touches down on the runway. You feel the wheels hitting the ground, and there is a loud noise as the pilot reverses the thrust of the engines. The plane begins to slow down, and you taxi toward the terminal.

The fear ladder for flying can also be used for boats, cars or trains. All you have to do is make up your own fear ladder using the basic outline. Substitute car, train, or boat for plane. Remember: *Always make the first scene the least scary, and the last scene the most scary.*

Now practice the relaxation tape at the end of the book and go through your fear ladder two steps at a time.

Even if you are not so scared of planes that you refuse to fly, you may, like most people, get knots in your stomach as you sit in the plane. If you find yourself getting nervous, try the relaxation exercises. As you sit in your seat, relaxing all the tension spots throughout your body, say silently to yourself, *"My thoughts are calm and clear."* This will help you to relax mentally and also keep your mind off the upcoming trip.

A phobia about flying can develop from a feeling of helplessness or lack of control over your own destiny. The dangers of flying and the trust you must place in the pilot are a lot like the dangers and uncertainties of life. You must have faith that everything will turn out all right. Some of your fear and tension in the plane might be an unconscious attempt to stop the plane from taking off, to control it. But of course you can't control the plane to that extent. You simply have to learn to relax and accept what is happening. In the same way, you can't always have complete control over events in your own life. Sometimes you have to be willing to let go and take risks, and have confidence in the future.

Claustrophobia, the fear of being shut in, is another reason for developing a fear of travel in a confined space, such as a car or plane. Gregory developed his fear of flying when he was about six years old. While playing in the garden one day with some friends in a small tent, his friends decided to tease him and wouldn't let him out of the tent. Just as he started to panic a plane flew very low overhead. He screamed until his friends released him. Although he didn't realize it at the time, his phobia toward flying had set in. He coupled his fear of being shut in the tent with an aircraft. It became more serious after he started dating a girl who lived near the scene of an air crash.

Gregory worked through the fear ladder using relaxation and imagining pleasant things in his mind between each scene. And sure enough, he overcame his fear sufficiently to fly out to California to visit his grandmother. But when it came time to return home he found he simply couldn't get on the plane. He had rushed through the fear ladder, without being sure to achieve at least four signs of relaxation at each step. He also needed some direct contact with airplanes and flying in a reassuring environment before he was able to conquer his fear.

Many people with flying phobias find it helpful to visit the airport and become familiar with all that is going on before they take a trip. Watching films about aircraft and flying can also be helpful, while you practice relaxation to remain calm. And some airline companies are giving courses to people with flying phobias to help them understand how the plane stays in the air, what all the various noises mean and why it is unreasonable to be afraid. The course usually winds up with a quick flight around the airport, with the pilot explaining in detail what he is doing and why.

If you hate flying and have to take a trip, find out if you can take such a course. It could be very helpful.

7
Nightmares and Things That Go Bump in the Night

It is normal for children to be afraid of the dark. Just about every three-year-old worries about seeing ghosts, monsters or robbers. Sometimes this is because when you are bad, you think about the punishment you deserve, and your fears multiply in the dark. You may also feel lonely in the dark and defenseless against danger, so your fear grows. Even adults prefer walking on lighted streets to walking on dark ones.

But as you get older, your parents probably won't listen to your bedtime fears. They say it's time you slept without a night-light, so gradually you learn to be ashamed of your fear and not to talk about it. Boys are particularly likely to pretend that they are no longer afraid of the dark. Unfortunately, as you've already seen, the less you talk about your fear the bigger it can grow.

Twelve-year-old Billy said his prayers every night before he went to sleep. But one phrase in particular made him worry—"if I should die before I wake." Thinking about this, he decided that every night he should tell God about all the bad things he'd done, just in case he died during the night.

But after he had thought of fifteen or twenty sins, it occurred to him that maybe he should say sorry twice. Then he worried that if he died before he got through with both lists, God wouldn't forgive him. So he began to speed up the two lists so that he wouldn't die in between saying them.

Then he wondered if perhaps God wasn't listening. Maybe he should write out his sins, so God could see that he was sorry while he was asleep. He remembered that in class he had to write out punishments twenty times. So he started writing out all his sins twenty times every night.

By this time, Billy wasn't getting much sleep and was worrying more and more about dying before God could forgive him. Billy had developed an obsession that made him act in a bizarre way to stop him from thinking about his fear of going to sleep. Many times when you are afraid of something, like Billy, you may find yourself thinking the same thing over and over again. You can't get it out of your head. This is a way people have of preventing fear from overwhelming them. But it's not a very effective way of behaving because it takes up so much time and energy.

If you find yourself thinking obsessive thoughts, or doing things over and over again to prevent yourself from getting scared, try this exercise:

OBSESSION EXERCISE

1. In the middle of your thoughts, shout out loud, *"Stop!"* Then, as you get used to obeying yourself, you will be able to say the word "stop" si-

lently, inside your head. It forces your mind to think about something else and stops the same thoughts from worrying you over and over.

2. Wear a rubber band around your wrist. Every time you start having fearful or repetitive thoughts, just twang the rubber band. It will hurt a little, but the pain will yank your attention away from your fear.

Mark, age nine, was having trouble getting enough sleep. Every night he would get up several times to fetch a glass of water, or call out in distress to his parents that he couldn't sleep. They became increasingly angry with him and decided he was just being silly. His marks at school started to suffer, and he didn't have enough energy to join in after school activities.

Eventually Mark's parents became worried and took him to a doctor. At first Mark denied there was anything wrong, but finally he admitted, "I try to go to sleep at night, but I just can't. Sometimes I stay awake all night long." But he wouldn't say why he was afraid. No, it wasn't the dark; no, it wasn't any noise; no, he wasn't afraid of wetting his bed.

Finally, Mark looked furtively around the room and blurted out, "It's the Manson gang. I'm afraid they're going to kill me."

It turned out that his older sister had told Mark that the Manson gang had been let out of prison and were roaming around, killing people. She warned Mark to keep his windows closed so they couldn't come to get him.

At this point Mark began to sob very quietly, distressed by the story he was telling. His sister admitted telling Mark the story, but said she had done it as a joke, just to scare him a little. But Mark had developed a fear of sleep, believing that if he were not on guard, the Manson gang would kill him.

As Mark talked it became clear that he was also very worried about his parents' real feelings toward him. Quite accurately, he felt that they were cold and hostile toward him. His parents had been divorced when he was only two, and he felt unloved by either one. He did not get on well with his stepfather, and his bad dreams were Mark's subconscious way of coping with his anger toward his parents over their lack of love, and his fear of being abandoned.

Mark needed to talk out some of his fear and anger with a therapist. He also learned to express his feelings toward his mother more and developed a closer relationship with her. In addition, Mark taught himself a simple relaxation exercise to help get rid of body tension and keep his mind off frightening thoughts.

BAD DREAM EXERCISE

1. Lie in bed with your eyes closed, breathing deeply.
2. Squeeze your left fist tight, then relax it.
3. Squeeze your right fist, then relax it.
4. Wrinkle up your forehead and try to tighten the muscles of your scalp and jaw. Relax. Feel the waves of relaxation as tension is released.

5.   Tighten the muscles in your left leg. Relax.
6.   Tighten the muscles in your right leg. Relax.
7.   Continue like this, repeating the contraction of muscles and relaxation. It will help distract your mind from frightening thoughts and relax your body so that you will have less difficulty falling asleep.

Now, turn to the back of the book and work through the fear ladder for sleep, using this relaxation exercise.

FEAR OF THE DARK

Rick's parents had just finished watching television. After turning out the lights and checking to make sure the doors were locked, they walked down a hallway to their room. On the right was Sally's room, where they stopped for a moment to make sure that she was covered for the night.

Across the hallway was Rick's room. When they opened the door, his parents found the light next to his bed was still on. His father walked over and turned it off. As he did this, Rick stirred in his sleep and woke up screaming.

Rick's parents were shocked. They didn't know what to think. Rick was twelve years old and for the past five years had slept without any type of nightlight. They couldn't understand this new development. Rick was very embarrassed by his parents' discovery, and at first he didn't want to talk about why he slept with a light on. "I like to read before I go to sleep and when I fall asleep, I forget to turn off the light," he told them.

His parents dropped the matter but checked his room each night for the next week. Each time, the light next to Rick's bed was on. They did not turn it off, but tried to decide what to do.

Rick's parents became increasingly concerned and went to a therapist to discuss the situation. Next, the therapist talked with Rick. The boy told him that his fear of darkness was very embarrassing and he didn't want anyone else to know about it. He said that every time the light was turned out, he would wake up, scared that something was going to happen in the dark, such as robbers breaking in.

Rick told the therapist that he first became scared when he saw a play on television in which a man was trying to kill a young boy trapped in a dark room. Since watching that play, he had grown more and more scared of being alone in a dark room. His fear grew so great that it turned into a phobia and even the thought of being in his room at night without a light would cause Rick to shake and tremble.

Since Rick had developed his fear from watching television, the therapist decided that he should not watch television for at least two hours before going to bed each night. He should also avoid watching shows with violent or frightening themes.

Then Rick and the therapist worked out a plan to help him overcome his fear of the dark.

PLAN FOR OVERCOMING FEAR OF THE DARK

1. For the first week, when Rick went to bed, he was to turn off the light and count to thirty slowly, then turn the light back on. He was to do this five times before he went to sleep, and then he could leave the light on all night. Each night, he was to add another count of thirty, so that by the end of the week he was counting up to thirty twelve times.

2. For the second week, when Rick lay down and was getting ready to go to sleep, he was to turn off the light, but instead of counting to thirty or more, he was to do the relaxation exercise listed at the end of the book. When he finished the exercise, he could turn the light back on. Rick was working at being relaxed with the light off.

3. As Rick went to sleep, he was to do his relaxation exercise until he could feel some of his fear disappearing. He was then to turn out the light and continue doing the relaxation exercises until he had calmed himself down. The door to his room was left open, with the hall light providing some light in his room.

4. Anytime during the night, if he woke up and started to become scared, he was to do his relaxation exercise.

   As a further help, Rick's father taped the relaxation session for him and let Rick have the tape recorder by his bed. If he should wake up in the middle of the night, he could reach over in the dark and turn on the tape recorder. The relaxation exercise on the tape recorder helped him get rid of his fear.

During the first few weeks, Rick was allowed to go around the house with his father and make sure that all the windows and doors were closed and locked. After the second week, Rick found that he did not need to do this anymore, since he trusted his father to close up the house properly.

Rick continued to work at pairing the relaxation exercise with his fear, and after a period of four weeks, he was able to sleep throughout the night without any lights on, and with his bedroom door closed.

8
The Two-Sided Fear: Failure and Winning

Throughout history, philosophers and scientists have talked about fear of the future and how people deal with it. Fear of failure is nothing more than fear that in the future we will be unhappy. Fritz Perls, a modern therapist, puts it another way:

"If we don't know whether we will get applause or tomatoes, we hesitate: the heart begins to race; all our excitement can't flow into activity, and we develop stage fright. So the formula for [fear] is very simple: the gap between the now and the then."

Anything that you anticipate in the future can be a source of fear. That's why you have to keep living in the present, because the moment you are experiencing right now is the only real one. Another writer has said: "We cannot change the past. We cannot truly deal with the future. The only moment we can give ourselves to is now."

Kent, age thirteen, was a good example of a boy who feared failing in the future. A nervous boy, he had been a chronic bed-wetter until he was eleven.

Medication did no good and after numerous consultations with urologists, the doctors concluded that Kent would simply grow out of it in time. The physicians stressed to Kent's parents that they should not punish him for bed-wetting, but be lavish with praise on those nights when he did not wet the bed.

At eleven years of age, when the bed-wetting stopped, Kent continued to develop normally, but other problems began to appear. Very slowly at first, Kent began making excuses to get out of going to classes. His father was a professor of economics at the local university and put a tremendous amount of pressure on his son to get good marks. He was constantly reminding him that if he didn't get good marks he would not be able to go to college and would be "doomed to a life of struggling to make a living."

Although Kent had been a B student before, now his marks dropped. At age thirteen, he was struggling to maintain a C average. His parents and teachers were at a loss to understand why Kent was having so much trouble. If only they had stopped to listen to him for a moment.

Because his parents had put such a do-or-die emphasis on getting good marks, Kent found himself becoming so nervous and anxiety-ridden before a test that he would forget the answers to the questions. Constant worrying about getting poor marks actually brought about his worst fears.

The situation had developed into a vicious cycle. The more anxiety-ridden he became, the poorer his marks were, and the more pressure his parents put on him to do better. He was developing a full-blown phobia toward school or anything to do with academic achievement. To top it all, he had started bed-wetting again, which only added to his anxiety. Phobias can often trigger a return to childish actions, such as bed-wetting if you are experiencing a lot of anxiety.

Fortunately, Kent's parents were willing to help Kent overcome his problems. They stopped putting so much pressure on their son, and Kent followed through with the following mental exercise:

SCHOOL, BAD MARKS PHOBIA EXERCISE

Nine Things to Tell Yourself When Fear Strikes

1. I'm going to keep my mind on the present, on what I have to do right now. My mind will not wander to the past or worry about the future.
2. I will label my fear from zero to ten (with ten being the worst) and in this way I can watch it lessen.
3. My fear will get worse only if I let it.
4. I will not try to eliminate my fear totally but will try to keep it manageable and at a comfortable level.
5. I can reason away my fear if I stop and think logically.
6. The problem will be over very soon if I don't allow it to scare me.
7. I try to think about something else.
8. I do something that will keep me from thinking about the fear (watching television, riding a bike, talking to a friend, etc.)

9. I look around me and focus my attention on other people who are not scared. I will become assertive with my fears.

In any competition there are winners and losers. And just as some people are afraid of losing, others are afraid of winning. Winning brings about its own changes and pressures. If you win once, you are expected to win again. Your parents and friends are counting on you. You can't let them down, right? Winning can be a little frightening, so some people never try as hard as they could. They are always coming in second, third or fourth. This way, they don't have to worry about the effects of winning.

Winning is not the most important thing in the world, and people who put winning above all else are usually unhappy people. Still, you should always try to do your best.

A racing-car driver had a problem. When he raced he usually led the field for most of the race, but when it came to the last few laps, he found himself letting up on the accelerator and going a little bit slower. Usually in the last lap another car would pass him and he would come in second or third. He was afraid of winning.

Lisa, age twelve, had a similar problem. She had been in gymnastics for almost three years and was thought to have an excellent chance of winning the events in which she participated. She could do almost anything on the beam during training. In gymnastics, ten is a perfect score. During training sessions, the coach told Lisa that most of her scores were between nine and ten. She was relaxed and confident about her abilities in these circumstances, but as soon as the real competition began, all Lisa could think about was the possibility of making a mistake and failing. Other thoughts also crossed her mind and confused her: "If I win this week, then I'll have to win next week, too. If I do well now, then everyone will expect me to do well whenever I get on the beam."

Lisa was afraid of success. Like most people, she was scared of a large crowd watching her and of making a mistake. But she was also fearful that if she won the event, everyone would expect her to win all the time. *She became fearful of winning!*

By using the relaxation exercises in this book, Lisa was able to overcome her fear of performing. But if she had not discovered that she also had a fear of winning, her performance still would not have been adequate.

You have seen two examples of people who had a fear of winning. Now let's examine some of the reasons why people do have this fear of winning. Think about yourself in a win-lose situation and see if any of these reasons for fear of success fit you: If I win, (1) everyone will stare at me, (2) people will think I'm showing off, (3) everyone will expect me to do it again, (4) I was told that girls are not supposed to win, (5) I'll hurt another person's feelings.

Do some of these thoughts occur to you when you are in a position to win? Perhaps you may be able to add statements to this list.

No one in the world can win at everything, every time they try. But there is a big difference between

84

those who try to win and are successful sometimes and sometimes come in second and third, and those who become so scared of winning that their nervousness prevents them from succeeding.

Work through the following fear ladder for success, using your relaxation exercises.

FEAR LADDER FOR SUCCESS

1. You find out that you are going to enter a competition or take a test.
2. You prepare for the upcoming event.
3. You feel slightly nervous as the day draws near.
4. As you prepare, you realize that possibly you are going to do a good job.
5. You become more nervous thinking about what is going to happen.
6. The day arrives and you wake up in the morning thinking about what is going to happen.
7. You begin to take the test, run in the race or compete in the event and you notice your nervousness diminishing at the beginning.
8. As things progress, you realize that you have a chance to do very well and your nervousness increases again.
9. You do the best in the class, or win the event.
10. People come up to you and say, "That's great—you can do it again next week. We knew you could do it all the time."

9
Fear of Death, Divorce, and Separation

The knowledge that you will die someday makes life that much more important. Some doctors feel that all fear and anxiety stem from our fear of death. Anything that threatens our survival makes us frightened.

Some people choose to avoid thinking about death by trying to escape. They turn to alcohol, or they are afraid to leave home, or grow up. They may always try to live close to their parents as a way of feeling secure. Some people are so frightened by the idea of growing old that they commit suicide. Their fear of death actually brings it about. If someone you love dies, you may feel guilty, fearing that something you did or bad thoughts you had about that person made him die. Or you may feel that you are being punished, that God is taking away someone you love because of something you did.

The same may be true if your parents get divorced. You experience a sense of loss, which is a kind of inner death. Your happy, close family is gone.

In a way, it has died. You may feel it is your fault, that something you did made your parents unhappy. Your parents may not be able to talk to you about it, because they are going through their own unhappiness, and realizing that you are unhappy makes them feel even more guilty about what they are doing.

But you have to find a way to discuss these feelings and discover how many of your fears are unfounded. Seek out good friends who will allow you to talk out your fears, and who will give you the support and reassurance you need. Otherwise, you will quite likely become depressed and unhappy.

You may worry about money. How will your parents pay all the bills? To make yourself feel more secure, you may start asking for presents. But this is the last thing your parents can afford right now, and they may become very angry with you for aggravating their own worries about money. So try to keep your fears under control. Your fears of becoming bankrupt and destitute are unlikely to come true.

Jane was so worried about being abandoned after her parents' divorce that she couldn't sleep at night. She was afraid that her mother would pack up her bags and leave her in the middle of the night. She was afraid that because she had been bad, neither of her parents wanted her anymore.

Sometimes, when parents fight a lot, children *want* one of them to leave, but this makes them feel guilty and they are afraid of being punished for their bad thoughts. Or children may feel they are the cause of trouble because of some expense or because of things that have been lost, destroyed or worn out—particularly if the parents quarrel about money, and they often do.

FEAR OF ABANDONMENT

Eddie's parents had divorced when he was five. Although he got on well enough with his stepfather and half-brother and -sister, he felt lonely and abandoned.

His stepfather was very strict and often tried to punish him, but his mother prevented it. Gradually, his stepfather stopped paying much attention to him. His mother had two smaller children to take care of and didn't have enough time for Eddie. He played hookey from school a lot, or complained of headaches and fatigue in order to stay home. Because he was away from school so much, he failed and had to repeat a grade.

Gradually, he became more rebellious. He started hanging out with older boys, staying out late, drinking, and getting into trouble. Eventually, Eddie was arrested for stealing and he was taken to a therapist for help.

Eddie was afraid of abandonment and loss of love from both his father and mother, who did not pay much attention to him. He acted the way he did in order to get attention, and his daring was actually a way of covering up his deep fear of being worthless and no good.

A feeling of being loved and of being worthwhile can stem from the knowledge that as a tiny baby you were well-loved by your parents. Before your memories began, they cherished you enough to take care of you and help you to grow up into the kind of person you are. From the secure knowledge that you have been loved in the past comes hope for the future. You can be reassured that any pain or unhappiness in the present will pass, and that you will be happy again.

If, like Eddie, you feel lost and unloved, try the following:

PLAN FOR FEELING SECURE AND LOVED

1. Sit down with your parents and ask them to tell you about your early childhood, which you were too young to remember.
2. Look through old family photographs showing how you looked as a baby and how you changed as you grew up.
3. Confide to your friends or your parents some of your fears and feelings about the future and the past. If they are true friends, they will help you feel better about yourself. "You aren't boring. Your good-looking date was vain and snobbish, and not worth your consideration."
4. Find out about your ancestors and your family history. Perhaps you will discover characteristics in some of your ancestors that you yourself possess—characteristics that will help you succeed in life.

5. Start a collection of "treasures." In time, just looking at this collection of things—coins, shells you have gathered at the beach, stamps, stickers, etc.—will remind you of happy experiences. It will help you remember that the future can be just as happy as the past.

Of course, you also need a feeling of security in the present—the feeling that your parents care about you enough to worry about where you are and what you are doing at all times. This can lead to arguments and nagging, as parents are just as fearful about your growing up as you are. You are changing very quickly before their eyes, and the changes make them feel uncomfortable because it means that pretty soon you will no longer need them. You will be truly independent and off on your own. They may feel they are losing you completely and feel abandoned by you.

But for the time being, you all need to learn to cooperate and live together harmoniously as a family. Fear often gets in the way of this and leads to angry outbursts and hurt feelings. Try doing the following:

FAMILY HARMONY EXERCISE

1. Write out a list of the things that are bothering you about your relationships with your family.
2. Now, on a second sheet, list all the things you like doing with your family—activities you enjoy, mealtimes, games you play together.
3. Sit down with your parents, and using the lists to

remind you of both sides of your feelings, try to discuss some of your complaints with them. Begin by telling them some of the things you enjoy, so they don't feel you are simply complaining.

4. Try to understand their point of view as well as your own. They are worried about you. Worry and fear can often be expressed as anger or disgust. They may take an attitude of, "We can't help you," while being very concerned and worried.

5. Tell them what you think is reasonable in the way of chores and responsibilities and what you would like in return—more allowance, more privacy, time to yourself, etc.

6. Work out a schedule of your activities, which you can paste up if you like. In this way, both you and your parents will know when you are supposed to be doing your homework, when you have agreed to baby-sit, and when you are free to go out.

You may be amazed that the number of family quarrels decreases dramatically. You may also feel much more secure and realize that your parents really do love you and are not just nagging you all the time.

10
Now It's Up to You

Having read this far, you know that while phobias are not simple things, they can be worked out and controlled with some effort on your part. However, many fears and phobias are so deeply ingrained that just working on reducing symptoms won't get rid of the underlying fear. If you have not been able to make the exercises work for you, don't get discouraged. Congratulate yourself that you have at least taken the first step in uncovering your fears. Then take the next big step: Seek out professional help. With the help of a psychologist or psychiatrist you can get to the bottom of your problems. Then you can use the exercises in this book to help get rid of your fears.

Let's review some of the basic principles of controlling the symptoms of fears and phobias. Some fears are necessary to help you survive. But if you spend a lot of time worrying about a particular thing or avoiding certain situations, your fear is becoming unreasonable and you need help to get rid of it. Think of your body reactions as clues to what frightens you. Do you ever have these fear symptoms?

BODY REACTIONS TO FEAR

1. Cold chills
2. Sweaty hands
3. Dry mouth
4. Upset stomach
5. Thumping heartbeat
6. Squeaky voice
7. Stuttering, difficulty talking
8. Feel like running away, but can't
9. Face feels hot
10. Hands shake
11. Knees weak and shaky
12. Shortness of breath
13. Blurry vision
14. Need to go to the bathroom
15. Gassiness
16. Lightheaded or dizzy feeling
17. Cold feet
18. Burping
19. Sweaty feet
20. Headache

Any one of these body signs can help you figure out what situations make you afraid. The more physical reactions you have, the more frightened you are, and the more you need to work on overcoming that fear.

Now, stand in front of the mirror and admit to yourself, "I am afraid of school," or whatever your fear may be. This will also help you uncover your fears. But be honest with yourself. Don't let fears build up by trying to keep them bottled up, or by ignoring them. Remember, that in order to overcome your fears it is enormously helpful if you can figure out why you are afraid, or when your fear first started. By gaining insight into the reason for your fear, you often realize that your life has changed since the fear began. You are no longer a small, helpless child. You now can do many more things for yourself that you could not do before. Even if some of your fear is due to unkind and cruel things your parents have done to you, you can, in time, learn to realize that you no longer need to be as afraid of them as you once were. Many of the things they did for you when you were a child you can now do for yourself, and pretty soon, you will be able to take care of yourself completely. But for now, concentrate on helping your body to relax and training yourself to think positively about situations in your life that frighten you. The following are some of the techniques you have learned throughout the book to help you overcome fear.

RELAXATION EXERCISES

1. Breathe in deeply, saying to yourself, "I am." Hold for five seconds. Breathe out, saying to yourself, "relaxed." Repeat five times.
2. Imagine yourself in a scary situation, such as taking a test at school. Practice your breathing exercise as you continue to imagine the scary situation. Feel yourself becoming more relaxed,

with a smile on your face. Imagine yourself finishing the test successfully and getting a good grade.

3. Just before giving a speech or performing in front of a group say to yourself, *"My thoughts are calm and clear."* Imagine yourself doing something you enjoy, such as reading a book, riding a bicycle, painting a picture, etc. Every time you feel panic rising, just repeat to yourself, *"My thoughts are calm and clear,"* and then imagine the enjoyable situation. Never run away from a frightening situation, unless you are in *real* danger. Think positively about yourself and always imagine yourself being successful in whatever you do.

4. Talk to someone you trust—a parent, teacher, or friend—about your fears. Realize that you are not alone. Everyone feels fear about the same kinds of things that you do. The more often you can face up to your fears and successfully overcome them, the easier it will become.

5. Learn to like yourself, as the first step in making friends. Make a list of all your attributes, both physical looks and accomplishments, and assure yourself that you are just as good as those around you. When you meet someone you would like to get to know, plan how you are going to do it. Write out a script of your meeting and all the things you will talk about. Practice in front of the mirror or with someone you trust. Practice your relaxation breathing while you are going through

with the planned meeting. Don't forget to smile! Congratulate yourself when you are successful. It helps build confidence and remind you that you can do it.

6. With your eyes closed, imagine a warm and pleasant situation, such as walking along a beach. Think of the word "calm" in your head as you relax in your pleasant scene. One by one, tighten, then relax the muscles of your stomach, back, chest, arm, forehead, scalp, around your nostrils, and jaw. Practice becoming completely relaxed for five minutes, three times a day.

7. Think of a situation that frightens you. Now break it down into ten steps, each one a little more scary than the last, or use the fear ladders at the back of the book. Write down each of the ten steps in the fear ladder on a separate index card. Practice remaining relaxed while you work through the stack of cards. Only attempt to work through two a day. Alternate thinking about the scene described in the card with relaxing thoughts about things you like to do. Practice with the cards three times a day.

8. Using the cards from the appropriate fear ladder, hold your breath for as long as you can. Have someone hold up a card in front of you as you gulp for breath. Work through your ten cards slowly, breathing deeply and holding your breath until you can feel relaxed throughout the fear ladder.

9. If you have a particular fear, such as a fear of dogs or insects, try clapping your hands or snap-

ping your fingers to break the fear habit. Or put a rubber band around your wrist and snap it each time you feel your fear coming on. The pain will distract your mind and stop you from thinking about your fear.

10. If you find yourself becoming obsessed with certain thoughts, thinking the same thing over and over again, shout to yourself, *"Stop!"* This will help stop the thought from recurring.

We have put the most important relaxation exercise at the back of the book because it is fairly long and you will need to read it over very carefully. Once you have read it, try to get a tape recorder and have someone you trust, someone with a soothing voice, read the exercise into the tape recorder. Then practice the exercise three times a day until you can relax at will.

If you are still having difficulty overcoming your fear, work out a plan with your parents or teacher to help you progress, little by little, toward conquering that fear. Don't be too ambitious. It is more important to succeed at small things than to attempt too much too quickly and fail. The experience of success is an important ingredient in teaching your mind to overcome fear. It feels good and you want more of it, so you will find yourself trying a little bit harder each time you succeed.

BEING ASSERTIVE WITH YOUR FEARS

As we have mentioned numerous times, it is extremely important for you to be assertive with your fears. This means adopting an attitude of saying to yourself, "I *can* do it."

When you are able to relax and think clearly, you should be able to act assertively on your fears.

What is assertive action? It can best be described as action that solves problems and makes you feel good about yourself and others. A person who acts assertively is neither passive nor aggressive.

A passive person is one like Tom in Chapter 3, who was afraid to mix with other children in the playground. He felt bad about himself—depressed, lonely, and angry. All of this made him feel that he had no control over his life and that he was incapable of solving his problems.

At the opposite extreme is Richard, in the same chapter, who was always showing off and calling others "scaredy-cat." He felt as bad about himself as Tom, but handled it by becoming aggressive. He bullied others, tried to make them look bad and picked quarrels with everyone. As a result, he ended up feeling just as lonely and angry as Tom.

Next time you get angry, ask yourself if the underlying reason may be fear. People often cover up their fear of being hurt or taken advantage of by lashing out at others. It may make you feel more powerful and prevent depression, but it's not a very effective way of getting what you want, because it makes others dislike you.

To summarize some of the helpful messages in this book, we have made a list of ten rules you should try to remember when you are faced with fear. They will help you relax, think in a clear, calm way about your predicament, and help you act in an assertive way.

TEN COMMANDMENTS FOR UNLEARNING YOUR FEARS

Whenever you are faced with fear, try to remember these ten commandments for unlearning your fears. They will help you relax, make a sensible decision, and act in an assertive manner.

1. Always remember that fears are messages you send yourself. Only you can change the message, like changing the channel on your television set.
2. Changing how you think and feel does not occur overnight. These types of changes take time. *You must be patient.*
3. You must be willing to admit your fears to yourself.
4. Don't be afraid to ask for help from parents, brothers, sisters, friends or professionals. Asking for help is nothing to be ashamed of, and it is an assertive way of overcoming fears.
5. Don't be discouraged and give up if a method doesn't work the first time. You may have to try several times before you succeed. People who fail and never try again are never very successful. Failure is a part of life, and you can learn a lot from it.
6. You *must* do your relaxation exercises every day.

Relaxation is like any other skill. The more you do it the better you get at doing it.

7. Don't let your fears snowball by pretending they do not exist. Very few fears will go away by themselves. Fears that are not resolved can lead to other fears.

8. Don't be scared just because you think other people expect you to be.

9. Know which of your fears are necessary to your well-being. Being scared of poisonous snakes, wild animals and swimming alone in the ocean may save your life.

10. Spend some time each day thinking about the things you do well, that make you feel good about yourself.

REAL-LIFE SITUATIONS

Once you have been able to master the relaxation exercises and the appropriate fear ladder, you are ready to attempt to face your fear in a real-life situation. If you are scared of dogs, or have a fear of flying, or a fear of darkness, then it is time for you to go up to the dog, take a flight, or sleep in a dark room, using your relaxation exercises and remembering how well you did with the fear ladder.

Act out the fear ladder in a real-life situation. But take your time and don't rush. You may want to take one step of the real-life fear ladder each day, moving slowly to allow for success at each step.

Check your body for signs of relaxation. Be sure you can achieve at least four of them while work-

ing through the fear ladder before you attempt to face
your fears in real life.

1. Arms and legs feel heavy
2. Breathing is slow and regular
3. Heartbeat is steady
4. Hands or feet tingle
5. You feel drowsy
6. Jaw feels heavy
7. Shoulders droop slightly
8. Sounds become distant

YOU'VE GOT THE KEY

You've now learned just about everything we
have to teach you about overcoming fears. But unfortunately we cannot do battle with your fears for you.
You must be willing to make the effort to practice
every day and to work hard at the relaxation exercises.

To help you make a commitment to overcoming
fears, we have drawn up a contract for you to copy and
sign. Read through it, then copy it on a separate
sheet and sign it, if you are truly committed to overcoming your fears. (*Do not write in this book.*)

CONTRACT FOR REDUCING YOUR FEARS

I,   commit myself to reducing my
fear reactions. I will be honest with myself about my
fears. I will learn the relaxation exercises. I will practice them every day, three times a day, until I have

mastered the ability to relax completely. I will continue to use relaxation in my daily life whenever I feel afraid.

If I should become discouraged, I will not give up, but will continue working on overcoming my fears.

Signed:

If you can do all these things, then you *will* be able to win the battle against your fears and you *will* be in control. Learning to cope with your fears and phobias will give you a taste of success, and once you realize that you have control over the way you act and the way you think, you can learn to be more confident about yourself and the way you behave with other people.

Now it's up to you, but don't hesitate to ask others for help. You may find that other people have the same fears and that you are not alone.

Here is your final checklist. On a separate sheet, put a mark beside each item as you complete it:

1. Read this book carefully.
2. Learn the relaxation exercises.
3. Practice the relaxation exercises three times daily.
4. Construct a fear ladder.
5. Use the fear ladder with the relaxation exercises.
6. Act out what you have learned in a real-life situation.

Good luck! And remember not to get discouraged if your fears seem overwhelming. Take them one at a time, and if you get bogged down, ask for help. You don't have to fight all your battles alone.

Appendix

You may read this out loud to yourself, have someone else read it to you, or best of all, have someone tape it for you. Then, whenever you need to relax, you can simply switch on the tape recorder.

Make yourself comfortable in a chair with a head-rest, or lie down. Let your arms rest by your side with your fingers open. Allow your eyes to close gently. Start recording.

Take a deep breath. Hold it. Now slowly breathe out and notice the tension in your chest begin to flow out as you exhale.

Once again, take a deep breath, hold it, slowly let it out. As your muscles begin to relax, you may start getting a pleasantly heavy feeling. If at any point during this exercise you get that pleasant heavy feeling anywhere in your body, let it flow. It's another way to get your muscles to relax.

Now tighten up your muscles and concentrate on the tension. Study where you feel the tension. Then relax and notice the different feeling when you relax. Start with the lower part of your body. Put your toes together pigeon-toed, heels slightly apart. Push your toes down away from you; this tightens your legs. Tighten your thighs, tighten your buttocks, tighten the muscles deep inside the buttocks. Study that tightness; hold that tightness. Tense. Tense. Tense. Now, slowly, let that tension go. Just relax and feel that tension flow out. Notice the muscles in your toes; relax them. Relax the muscles of your legs; let them go. Relax your thighs, relax those deep muscles. Relax. Slowly, gradually, notice the tension flowing out of your legs.

Now work the muscles of your abdomen. Tighten up your abdominal muscles as if a little boy were going to push a football into your stomach. Just get them tight. Study where you feel the tension, hold it. Tense. Tense. Tense. Now, slowly, let that tension flow out from your abdominal muscles. Feel them become loose, limp, and relaxed. Notice the feeling of tension flowing out and the feeling of relaxation flowing into the muscles of your abdomen. Now try to relax the muscles deep in the abdomen, the muscles of your stomach and intestine.

With your stomach muscles relaxed, focus your attention on the muscles of your back. Arch the small of your back and get tension in there. As you arch, there are two long columns of muscles, one on each side of your spine. That might be where you feel it. Wherever you feel it, get to know it. Hold it. Tense. Tense. Tense. Now let go. Just relax the muscles of your back, letting them go. Try to let your back just melt into the chair, more and more relaxed. With your back relaxed, focus your attention on the muscles of your chest.

Take a deep breath through your mouth, and hold it. As you hold it, you may notice spots of tension building up in your chest. If you do, take note of them. Remember where they are and keep holding. Now, as slowly as you can, let it out. At the end, breathe easily and comfortably, the way you do in a deep sleep. If you have noticed spots of tension in your chest, take them a spot at a time and let them go. Relax those muscles of your chest, just keep relaxing them. Think of each part as it is mentioned.

Abdomen relaxed. The muscles in your stomach and intestine relaxed. Feel your back relaxed; let it melt into the chair. Feel your chest relaxed as you breathe easily and comfortably, the way you do in a deep sleep. Now with these muscles relaxed, focus your attention on your left forearm and hand.

Clench your left hand in a fist as tightly as you can. Feel that tension in your left hand and forearm as you clench very tightly. Tense. Tense. Tense. Now, slowly, allow that tension to flow out of your left hand and forearm. Notice how different it feels as you relax your left hand and forearm. Very gradually, let the tension drop off. Your forearm is becoming very loose, limp and relaxed. Let it get as relaxed as it possibly can. Now keeping your left forearm and hand relaxed, focus your attention on your right forearm and hand.

105

Clench your right forearm and hand into a very tight fist. Tense. Squeeze till you feel that tension, that tight cramped feeling. Now release it slowly. Focus carefully on the way it feels. What does it feel like to you as that tension flows out of your fingers, as your fingers spread out? They seem to feel like they're getting longer and longer. Very slowly, relax, gradually, very surely, relaxing fingers and forearm as the muscles in your forearm and fingers become very soft and relaxed. Now keeping your right forearm and hand relaxed, shift your attention to your left hand.

Place it palm down on the chair and press as hard as you can. Press tight, tight. Feel that tension in the upper part of your left arm. Feel it tighten. Now, slowly, let it become relaxed. Notice your whole left arm becoming very, very heavy. As relaxed as you can possibly go, allow that left arm, slowly, to become more and more relaxed. Notice the difference of this relaxed feeling. Compare it with what it felt like just a minute ago when it was tense. Very surely, very gradually, feel the left arm becoming more and more relaxed. With your left arm relaxed, focus your attention now on your right hand.

Press your right hand down on the chair arm very hard. Tense. Tense. Feel that pressure in the upper part of your right arm. Tense. Now, slowly, let that tension out. Allow your right arm to become more relaxed. Focus on the way your arm feels as you let that tension drain away. Notice that your arm becomes very loose, limp and relaxed and your whole right arm becomes very relaxed and very heavy. Check for any tension in your left and right arms. If you notice any leftover tension, allow that, too, to gradually, surely flow out.

Now work with the shoulders. The best way to do this is by keeping your lower arms relaxed while shrugging your shoulders and dragging your shoulders up to your ears. Now, shrug your shoulders very hard—hold that tension—feel that cramped sensation behind your neck and in the upper part of your back. Now slowly relax and allow your shoulders to come down. Allow that tension to flow out. Notice the relief as the tension flows out and relaxation takes its place. Allow your arms and shoulders to become very relaxed. Now focus on the muscles between your shoulder blades and the muscles in the back of your neck and head.

These are muscles that are very sensitive to tension. Pull your shoulders back so your shoulder blades are almost touching and at the same time press your head back into the back of the chair or mattress. Feel that cramped sensation in the back of your neck and shoulders. Hold it. Tense. Tense. Now slowly let the tension go. Relax those muscles in the back of your neck and between your shoulder blades. Let them go. Allow those neck muscles to become so loose, so limp, and so relaxed that they are no longer supporting your head and your head falls limply back to the pillow, more and more relaxed.

Now focus your attention on the delicate muscles of your face. We'll start with the upper part. Squeeze tight the upper part of your face. Squeeze your eyes tightly shut. Wrinkle the bridge of your nose. You feel the tension in your forehead and scalp, between your eyebrows where you frown and in the cheeks under your eyes. Hold it. Tense. Tense. Tense. Now relax and feel that tension flowing out. Relax the muscles of your forehead and scalp. Let them go. Relax the muscles between your eyebrows where you frown. Relax your eyelids. As they relax, they may begin to feel heavy. You may start getting a pleasant sleepy feeling. But don't go to sleep. The aim is to get your body relaxed and keep your mind awake and alert and in control. Relax the muscles on the bridge of your nose. Let them go. Relax the cheeks under your eyes where they feel tight.

Now the muscles in your jaw and tongue. Squeeze your back teeth together so you get your jaw good and tight. Feel your jaw tight. You feel it by your temples, by your ears. Now keeping your jaw tight, push with your tongue against the back of your bottom front teeth so your jaw is tight and your tongue is tight. Tense. Tense. Tense. Now relax. Let go. Allow the tension to flow out. Allow the muscles of your jaw to relax. Relax your tongue. You will probably find your teeth parting slightly, your jaw hanging slack, more and more relaxed.

Now the lower part of your face. Make a grin showing your upper and lower teeth and pulling the corners of your mouth back. You feel the tension by your nostrils, around your mouth and chin. Hold it. Tense. Tense. Now relax. Allow the tension to slowly, flow out of your muscles, feeling more and more relaxed. Relax those muscles around your mouth and chin.

Now try to relax the muscles of your throat, the soft part of your throat, where you swallow. Relax those. Relax the muscles around your voice box. More and more relaxed.

Now it is time to terminate the relaxation exercise. Count down slowly from three to one, and at the count of one, open your eyes and sit up. "Three, two, one. Hello, world!" Flex your arms, flex your legs, and get up.

The following fear ladder exercises work best if you write down each step on a separate index card. This will help you to concentrate and to imagine each scene or situation vividly.

FEAR LADDER FOR HEIGHTS

1. There is a ladder raised against the side of a building. You look at the ladder and let your eyes travel up the side of the building.
2. You walk over to the ladder and put your foot on the first rung. Then you put both feet on the first rung, holding the sides of the ladder with your hands. You stand there for a few moments, then proceed up to the next rung.
3. You are now halfway up the ladder and looking up toward the top.
4. You climb a little bit higher, then look down. You focus on the ground and look to your right and to your left.
5. You are standing outside a very tall building and slowly look up all the way to the top.

6. The elevator carries you to the upper floors of the building. You arrive at the fifteenth floor and leave the elevator.
7. You walk toward a window. As you get closer to the window, you can see the sides and tops of other buildings.
8. You are at the window and look out and down. Below you the people, cars, and sidewalks look very, very small.
9. You open the glass doors and walk out onto a balcony. All around you is open sky, and you walk toward the railing which surrounds the balcony.
10. Placing both hands on the railing, you lean your head over slightly and look down toward the ground.

FEAR LADDER FOR SLEEP

1. You are watching television and there is an advertisement for beds.
2. It is getting late in the day and you begin thinking about going to bed.
3. You look out the window and it is dark.
4. Your mother tells you that it is almost time to go to bed.
5. You walk into your bedroom and look down at your bed.
6. You sit down at the edge of the bed and turn out the light.
7. The room is completely dark as you put your head back on the pillow.

8. You close your eyes and breathe in and out, deeply and slowly.
9. You lie there with your eyes closed, listening for sounds in the room.
10. The room is quiet, your eyes are closed, and your breathing is deep and regular. You are going to sleep . . . you are asleep.

FEAR LADDER FOR NIGHT

1. You see the word "night" written in large black letters on a piece of paper.
2. A friend tells you it is going to be a nice, dark night.
3. You look out your window and notice that the sun is beginning to go down.
4. You have to turn on the lights in the house because it is becoming dark.
5. As you look out the window, everything is hidden by darkness.
6. It is two o'clock in the morning and you can hear sounds of insects outside the house in the darkness.
7. You see yourself standing by the window looking out into the darkness.
8. You open the door and begin to step out into the darkness.
9. You are outside your house. It is dark around you, except for the light coming from the open door.
10. The door closes behind you and you remain in complete darkness outside your house. You stand there for five minutes.

FEAR LADDER FOR ASKING A QUESTION

1. You are sitting at your desk at school.
2. The teacher is explaining a mathematics problem which you do not understand.
3. There will be a test on this type of problem tomorrow.
4. You are afraid of getting bad marks.
5. The teacher asks if there are any questions.
6. You begin to raise your hand, but you are afraid that the question will seem foolish.
7. The teacher calls on you and you ask the question.
8. Students next to you giggle and you think they are laughing at your question.
9. The teacher begins to answer your question.
10. You still do not understand one part of the answer, and you ask the teacher to explain in more detail.

FEAR LADDER FOR INSECTS

Note: The word "insect" is used to describe any type of insect, spider or very small creature. You should substitute the particular insect of which you are afraid. Only non-poisonous, harmless insects or spiders should be used in this ladder!

1. The person sitting behind you tells you that there is an insect on the floor next to your foot.

2. You look down and see that the insect is about two feet away from you.
3. The insect is crawling toward you.
4. The insect is getting closer and you feel like yelling and running away.
5. The insect changes direction and begins crawling next to your desk, not toward your feet.
6. You look down and can see the insect very clearly.
7. The insect changes direction again and comes back toward your feet.
8. The insect is only a foot away.
9. The insect is only four inches away.
10. You move your feet and the insect crawls past.

FEAR LADDER FOR INJECTIONS

1. The doctor tells you you need an injection.
2. You look around his office and see the needle as it is being filled.
3. The doctor or nurse puts some alcohol on your arm with a little cotton swab, cleaning off the area to be injected.
4. They tell you to hold really still.
5. You see the needle and syringe as they bring it closer to your arm.
6. You look away and feel the pin prick as the needle goes into your arm.
7. You feel the sting as they give you the injection.
8. They pull out the needle.

9. They wipe the area again with some alcohol-soaked cotton.
10. You look down and see the needle after the doctor has used it.

FEAR LADDER FOR DENTISTS

1. Your parents tell you it's time to go to the dentist.
2. You're in the car on the way to the dentist's office.
3. You're in the dentist's waiting room and the nurse calls your name.
4. You're sitting in the dentist's chair and he is examining your teeth.
5. He's checking your teeth with his tools and he takes some X rays.
6. The dental hygienist helps clean your teeth.
7. The dentist gives you an injection so that he can fill your cavity.
8. You can hear and feel the drill as he's fixing your cavity.
9. He uses tools to clean out the cavity.
10. He puts the filling into your tooth.

FEAR LADDER FOR BOYS GOING OUT ON A DATE

1. On Monday you asked Sue to go to the Saturday night school dance.
2. You have to pick her up at six o'clock and you've just finished getting dressed.

3. You worry about being embarrassed because your father has to drive you.
4. You wonder if everyone will laugh at you if you can't dance very well.
5. You're not sure what to talk about.
6. You're starting to feel more anxious as your father tells you it's about time to leave.
7. You get into your father's car and ride to her house, where your father parks and you walk up to the door.
8. You ring the doorbell and she answers the door.
9. You talk with her parents for a little while and then leave.
10. Back at the car, you introduce her to your father and leave for the dance.

FEAR LADDER FOR GIRLS
GOING OUT ON A DATE

1. On Monday, Tom called you on the telephone and asked if you would go to the Saturday night school dance with him.
2. He will be at your house at six o'clock and you look at the clock and see that it is five-thirty and you're not ready yet.
3. You've finished dressing and are beginning to feel nervous.
4. You try to imagine what you can talk about during the dance.
5. You wonder if he is going to try and kiss you.

6. You're worried that your dress may be old-fashioned.
7. You hear the doorbell ring.
8. You open the door and there's Tom.
9. He meets your parents and you talk for a little while.
10. You leave for the dance and have a wonderful evening.

FEAR LADDER FOR THUNDER AND LIGHTNING

1. The sky begins to get cloudy and its feels like rain.
2. The rain starts to fall, a very light rain at first.
3. You look up in the sky and the clouds are beginning to get darker and the rain is getting heavier.
4. There is a distant roar of thunder.
5. Lightning can be seen lighting up the sky in the distance.
6. You look up in the sky and see the lighting is getting closer and the thunder is sounding nearer.
7. Each strike of lightning illuminates the whole sky and the thunder seems to shake the ground.
8. Each clap of thunder gets closer to the next and the lightning is more frequent.
9. The rain is very heavy now and it blocks your view for any distance.
10. The thunder and lightning are directly overhead and the storm is at its full force.

FEAR LADDER FOR GIVING A
SPEECH IN FRONT OF YOUR CLASS

1. Your teacher has just told you that you will have to give a speech in front of the class.
2. You prepare the speech at home and do all the necessary reading and writing.
3. The day of the speech arrives and it will be your turn next.
4. The teacher calls your name and you come up to the front of the classroom.
5. You look out at all of your classmates and see that most of them are looking at you.
6. You have your notes in front of you and your hands are sweaty and you're nervous.
7. The teacher tells you to begin your talk and you do.
8. As you're giving your speech, you look up on occasion and see all of the people in the classroom watching you.
9. You're coming to the end of your speech and must remember how you are going to finish.
10. You have finished your speech and now the class is going to ask you questions.

Selected Readings

Fensterheim, Herbert J. and Jean Baer. *Stop Running Scared*. New York: Dell, 1978.

Janov, Arthur. *The Feeling Child*. New York: Simon & Shuster, 1973.

Klein, Carole. *The Myth of the Happy Child*. New York: Harper & Row, 1975.

Olshan, Neal and Julie Wang. *Phobia Free and Flying High*. New York: Condor, 1978.

Wolman, Benjamin B. *Children's Fears*. New York: Grosset & Dunlap, 1978.

Wood, John. *What Are You Afraid Of?* New Jersey: Prentice-Hall, 1976.

Index

Abandonment, 1–2, 75, 87, 88–90
Adrenaline, 4
Aggression, 35–37, 98
Airplanes, 66–71
Animals, 56–65
Assertive action, 97–99
Authority figures, 3
Avoidance, 10–13

Bed-wetting, 80
Bees, 57–59
Blood pressure, 5, 14
Blood tests, 52
Boats, 66, 67, 69
Breathing exercises, 15–16, 54–55, 94, 103

Cars, 66, 67, 69, 70
Cats, 7–8

Claustrophobia, 70
Competition, 12, 13, 83–85
Confidence, 8, 22, 31, 32
Crying, 40, 52–53
Cultural conditioning, 56–57

Darkness, 72, 76–79
    fear ladder for, 111
Dating, 39
    fear ladder for boys, 114–115
    fear ladder for girls, 115–116
Death. See Dying
Dentists, 53–55
    fear ladder for, 114
Divorce, 86–87
Doctors, 44–53

Dogs, 13, 59–64
Dreams, bad, 75–76
Dying, 72–73, 74–75, 86

Embarrassment, 23

Failure, 12, 13, 80, 99
Family counseling, 45
Family relationships, 45–46, 75, 86–91
Fears
    admitting, 41–42
    avoiding, 10–13
    body reactions to, 4–5, 7, 14–15, 93
    contract for reducing, 101–102
    identifying, 9–10
    list of, 9–10
    origins of, 3–4, 94
    outgrowing, 5, 57
    therapy for, 6, 21–22
    unlearning, 16, 49–51, 99–100
Feelings, deep, fear of, 13
Fight-or-flight response, 4–5
Flying, 66–71

Friends, making, 31–40
    exercise for, 37–39
Future, 80

Growing up, 39–40, 86

Heights, 3–4
    fear ladder for, 109–110
Heroes, 33
Hobbies, 34
Hospitalization, 51–53
Hyperventilation, 55
Hypochondria, 43

Illness phobia, 43–55
Infants, fears of, 1–2
Injections, 44, 51
    fear ladder for, 113–114
Insects, 57–59
    fear ladder for, 112–113
Insecurity, 18–19

Lightning, 116
Losing, 83
Love, lack of, 88–91

Money, 87–88

120

Mother, separation from, 1–2

News media, 67
Night, 111
Nightmares, 45

Obsessions, 3, 73
    exercises for, 73–74, 97
Oedipus complex, 3

Parents
    approval from, 36, 37
    child's fear of, 3
    child's love of, 3
    insecurities of, 45–46
Passivity, 98
Performing, 95
Perls, Fritz, 80
Phobias, defined, 1. *See also* Fears
Physical education class, 13
Physical examination, 48–49
Popularity, 34
Psychiatrists, 6

Question asking, 112

Rejection, 13
Relaxation, 5–6, 8, 15–16
    exercises, 46–47, 62–63, 94–97
    signs of, 64–65
    tape recorded exercise, 46–48, 78–79, 103–109
Ridicule, 13, 21, 25, 35, 36, 60

School phobias, 18–30
    exercises for, 24–25
    grades, 80–83
Security, 88–91
Self-confidence, 8, 22, 31, 32
Self-esteem, 20, 31–34
Shots. *See* Injections
Showing off, 35–37, 98
Shyness, 35, 40, 58
Sick (Silverstein), 29
Silverstein, Shel, 29
Sleep phobias, 72–79
    fear ladder for, 110–111

Speech giving, 7, 13, 25, 26, 27
    fear ladder for, 117
Strangers, 2
Stuttering, 7, 25–27
    exercise for, 27–28
Success, 83–85
Suicide, 86
Survival instinct, 4–5

Talents, 34
Television, as cause of fears, 45, 57, 62, 67, 77

Tests, 7, 13
Therapy, 6, 21–22
Thunder, 116
Timidity, 35, 58
Trains, 66, 67, 69
Travel, 66–71

Ulcers, 5, 14

"Where the Sidewalk Ends," 29
Winning, 83–85